LIBRARY OF THE EARLY CIVILIZATIONS
EDITED BY PROFESSOR STUART PIGGOTT

The Warring States of Greece

THE WAR

FROM THEIR RISE TO

McGraw-Hill Book

RING STATES OF GREECE

THE ROMAN CONQUEST

A. R. Burn

Company · New York

DESIGNED AND PRODUCED BY THAMES AND HUDSON

LIBRARY OF CONGRESS CATALOG CARD NUMBER: 68–27531
PRINTED IN GREAT BRITAIN
09180

CONTENTS

GENERAL EDITOR'S PREFACE

When in Europe, from the end of the Middle Ages onwards, the ancient Greeks were being seen through scholarly spectacles of various tints, their long history of petty warfare and their occasional major encounters were viewed, with other aspects of Hellenic culture, within the framework of successive changes in fashionable ethics and politics. Once Classical culture was thought of as an exemplar, each generation constructed an ancient Greece for itself embodying the qualities thought most socially desirable at the time, and therefore 'good', while the unfamiliar and alien traits were played down as 'bad'. The process, of course, continues today, in so far as every historian and age creates an individual past, but we no longer feel the necessity for making the Greeks paragons living in a Golden Age that is a product of our wishful thinking, and aspects once felt to be embarrassing – slavery, pederasty, warfare aggressive or internecine – can be accommodated in a view of Greek culture hardly possible in the past.

Mr Burn has deliberately selected for discussion in this book that aspect of the ancient Aegean in which it appears as a little world of warring states. This phrase can in turn be used to convey a reference to China between the Chou and Ch'in dynasties, from the eighth to the third century BC, and so contemporary with the scope of the book: a reminder that the Greek world was only one of several civilizations within this period. With one of these, the Persian, Greece came into memorable conflict at an early date; in the West, Greek colonists encountered the Etruscans; under Alexander, Greek power was extended into the heart of the ancient Near East from Egypt to India. Elsewhere the Greeks encountered barbarians, in whose territories it was possible to establish colonies, from the Black Sea to Spain, among Thracians, Scythians, Celts or Iberians, to say nothing of the ancient inhabitants of Italy and Sicily.

The city-states of ancient Greece were the product of an economy based, as the ancient world of civilized peoples and barbarians alike was everywhere based, on mixed agriculture at a level of competence which enabled not only permanent settlement in village or town, but provided a surplus which could be used to provision specialized non-productive sections of the population, such as an army in the field. The military grain ration, in Greece as in the Roman world, was about ten bushels per head per annum, which was roughly the yield of an acre of crop in Classical antiquity as in the Middle Ages, and only with such an assured levy could warfare develop beyond the tip-and-run raids of those with a less organized food-supply. Policy could only be framed to satisfy those real or assumed needs of the city-states which were thought to be capable of solution by warfare, so long as there was a carbohydrate (and less a protein) constituent of diet available for distribution.

Agriculture was therefore one of the technologies which could be exploited to supply the forcible implementation of state decisions, and the other, of course, was metal-working. The skilful use of bronze had been known in the Aegean since early in the second millennium BC, and from about the tenth century BC the quite different techniques of iron-working had been acquired. It was therefore possible to produce a soldiery adequately equipped with defensive armour and offensive weapons capable of holding its own not only in internecine quarrels, but in conflict with other, non-Greek, peoples at a comparable technological level.

The early Greek foot-soldier was equipped with plate-armour of helmet, corselet and greaves; armed with spears and javelin, and protected by a round shield, the *hoplon*, which gave its name to the drilled phalanx of infantrymen, the hoplites, as war became more disciplined. Archilochos, that splendid seventh-century poet, randy bastard of a Parian nobleman, turned mercenary, escaped by abandoning his –

> When the fighting grew hot.
> Life seemed somehow more precious.
> It was a beautiful shield
> I know where I can buy another,
> Exactly like it, just as round.

The cynical shrug of the shoulders carries far more conviction than the oratory of general or politician. This is what war consists of.

The history of Greek armour is bound up with that of the bronze-working techniques not only of the Aegean but of barbarian Central Europe in the first millennium BC, and a sinister figure in armour alien to the ancient Oriental world swaggers into the Old Testament narrative in the person of the Philistine Goliath, armed with helmet, corselet, greaves and shield, and carrying a throwing-spear so odd that the Hebrew writer could only liken it to the leash-rod of a loom with its side-loop. This must have been a javelin thrown with a loop of cord in the early Greek manner, a device allied to the spear-throwers of Upper Palaeolithic man and recent primitive hunters, but so familiar to the Greeks that Strabo thought it worthy of comment that the Celtic Belgae of the second century BC did *not* use this technique.

Greek military power then was essentially based on the armoured, shield-bearing, spear-wielding, infantryman; swords were also used but archery was always a foreign idea, regarded as unworthy of a gentleman, and left in the hands of mercenaries such as Cretans or Scythians, the latter particularly being employed in Athens by Pisistratos. All this equipment needed not only iron and bronze, but craftsmen skilled in the by no means simple technological expertise of making such objects as one-piece helmets, and behind warfare, as always, lay the armaments industry. It was at no higher standard of competence than that of contemporary barbarians, let alone that of the more civilized adversaries of Greece. All its basic techniques and processes had as we saw been worked out many centuries before so far as bronze-working was concerned, and since the Greek Dark Ages in respect of iron. It sufficed in a small world of small wars, and later in the more extended annexations of Alexander. Wars are the physical outcome of extreme psychological tensions involving concepts of honour and the demonstration of valour in approved forms and, provided the necessary catharsis is achieved, scale is irrelevant.

STUART PIGGOTT

INTRODUCTION

Amid all the rich variety of the growth of civilization in different parts of the Old World, there are some striking similarities; and of these, none is more remarkable than the fact that it is in or about the sixth century BC that, alike in China and India and in Western Asia, from Persia to the eastern part of the Greek world, some men began to question or reject the religions of the Bronze Age and to express thoughts, widely differing in character, which we, their descendants, still find relevant to the human predicament today. This Axis Age, as the German scholar Karl Jaspers has called it, is thus only about eighty generations before our time, a small matter in the million-year history of our species. So young is our civilization; a fact which we may well find cheering in the circumstances of our own stormy and puzzled age.

In our western world, the contributions of Greece and Israel are still basic to all that has been done since. That of Greece, the subject of this book, includes both its art and architecture, influential in the west since their rediscovery in the last five hundred years, its poetry and history, the categories of our philosophers and, most important of all, the first adumbrations of the physical and social sciences. These are the subjects of other volumes in this series. Our special concern here is with the political and social development of that Greek world in which so much was achieved.

It was not the achievement of a world peace. Indeed, in moral philosophy and in the surviving fragments of the moralizing poetry which preceded it, we can see clearly that it was the instability and the injustices of society that stimulated reflection. This was the case too, with Confucius and his contemporaries in China, with Gautama the Buddha in India and with Zarathustra (Zoroaster) in Persia. The age into which Confucius was born is known, in the Chinese historical tradition, as the Age of the Warring States. And, both in east and west, the age ended with the absorption of the states by conquering empires: the Han Empire, Rome, and in India the less durable Mauryas. The peace-making achievement of the empires was impressive, and its memory long-lasting; but in purely intellectual matters, none of these more stable states was nearly as brilliant as the stormy society that had gone before.

A. R. B.

CHAPTER ONE

After Mycenae

The historical Hellenic civilization did not start directly from Neolithic village life. Here as in Asia, though Greek tradition preserved but faint memories of it, there had been since the third millennium BC a high and artistic Bronze Age civilization, with centres, among which Knossos in Crete may fairly be called a city, where royal families and their retainers lived in considerable luxury; the civilization described in this series by Sinclair Hood in *The Home of the Heroes*. In its later and warlike phase, when the residence of its most powerful kings was in the mainland fortress of Mycenae, the Greek-speaking chiefs of the peninsula were capable of uniting under their High King for large-scale military or raiding enterprises. The siege of Troy (*c.* 1200 BC?), remembered in Greek poetry, may have been one of the last of them. 'Ahhiawan' marauders, whose name recalls the Achaians of Homer, had, even before this, molested the west coast of the Hittite Empire in Asia Minor. Allied with the chariot-driving Libyans of Cyrenaica, and with other sea-peoples, perhaps of the Asia Minor coasts, they threatened Egypt in 1221 and 1194 and may have taken part in the overthrow of the Hittite power about 1200. But their piracy, cattle-raids and wars, which were more frequently small-scale affairs against each other, weakened them and destroyed the once far-flung Mycenaean and Levantine trade. The costliness of armour and the gulf between the palace people and peasants, to which both archaeology and, much later, Homer bear witness, suggest that among them first-class warriors must have been relatively few. In these circumstances it is easy to believe the Greek story, that the grandsons of the captors of Troy were overrun by rougher Greeks from the north, the Dorians and others, whose society, we may guess, was still tribal, with every man a warrior. There is also a current theory that the abandonment of many late Mycenaean sites, together with increased occupation of the more rainy western islands, eastern Attica and some eastern islands, was due to a temporary climatic fluctuation producing a prolonged drought. In this case the Dorians and other north-western Greeks will merely have moved in later, when rainfall increased again, into an almost deserted region. This, however, was not what the Greeks believed.

A Dark Age

The fall of the Mycenaean palaces, like the collapse of Roman government in the west later, was followed by a 'dark age'. The contact with the Levant, which enables us to date the phases of Mycenaean civilization, is broken after 1200 BC; the burned palaces lay in ruins and deserted, some of them, as at Pylos, to the present day; and while invaders or survivors may have built their huts near by, the remains of their much poorer settlements have in many areas not yet been discovered. But it may be premature to say that whole areas, previously settled, were left uninhabited. Absence of evidence (so far) is not evidence of absence. Dr Rhys Carpenter suggested that a minor climatic fluctuation reduced the rainfall below the level sufficient for agriculture; but this seems not to account for the fact that in eastern Attica, as well as the wetter western islands, Mycenaean ways lasted longer.

1 The oldest masonry open to view on the Acropolis (to the right, from the top of the way up) is that of these remains of what Classical Athens called the Pelargic Wall or Fortress. (The remains of the covered way to a water supply, the wooden steps fitted into a cleft in the northern cliff, were dangerous and have been covered up.) In the photograph, the Parthenon rises dramatically behind foundations of the wall that protected an earlier Athens

On the positive side, what can be seen is that before 1000 BC and probably first at Athens, which, with her strong Acropolis and Late Mycenaean covered way to a water-supply, had outridden the storm, there are clear signs of returning social vitality. The tokens of this are the pottery decorated in the style known as Protogeometric; pottery, surviving as usual even if in fragments, where textiles have perished and metal-work has, for the most part, been melted down; pottery decorated in a strong, simple style, a folk style, which has been hailed as the first truly Hellenic art. It is the art of a still poor, but intelligent and vigorous population, emancipated, not

Ill. 1

Ills 2, 3

2, 3 An end and a beginning: the chariot craters of Late Mycenaean Cyprus continue to emphasize, though with decreasing artistic competence, the pride of the 'palace people', local kinglets and chiefs, in that aspect of their privileged status which was most easily depicted. The new Protogeometric art, which arises at Athens perhaps about 1025 BC, abstract, restrained, content with simple designs and not even, like later Geometric, insisting on filling every empty space, has been hailed as the first Hellenic artistic style

without much destruction and misery, from the rule of the palace-dwellers and the prestige of their overripe Mycenaean art.

The Protogeometric and the many local schools of mature Geometric art which evolved from it had, altogether, a career of over three centuries. The phases, in the absence of writing (an art which had been lost in the great wreck) and of contact with the still literate east, are difficult to date; but from its increase in quantity in the later phases, we can trace the slow process of consolidation, and infer that the population was increasing again. Protogeometric pottery found at old Smyrna must have been brought by settlers – the first Greeks to cross the Aegean north to the mainland settlements which, with the island of Lesbos, became known as Aeolis. Ionia, with Chios and Samos, came a little later; then Asian Doris, with the peninsular cities of Cnidus and Halicarnassus, and Rhodes and Cos, islands, which, unlike the

Ill. 4

others, are represented as already Greek (Pre-Dorian?) in Homer's Catalogue of the fleet at Troy. The Cyclades also, unmentioned in Homer's Catalogue, were Greek in time to have their own schools of Geometric art; and their people in historic times spoke dialects akin to those of Ionia and of Attica and Euboea, from which many of the colonists of Ionia were believed to have come.

South of these, stretching from the kingdoms of Argos, Sparta and Messenia in the Peloponnese, in a wide arc through Crete and the southernmost islands to the Asian Doris, lay the Dorian states, founded according to tradition by the North Greek invaders who had sacked Pylos and Mycenae. The tradition appears to be sound. Throughout this area the populations are found divided into the same three Doric 'tribes' (sometimes together with others, founded to include pre-Dorian survivors). They spoke varieties of a common Doric dialect, more archaic than the Ionic, and marked, for instance, by the broad ā sound (as in *father*), which in Ionic changed to E (French è or ê). In the central Peloponnese, in highland Arcadia, by-passed by the invaders, there survived a still more archaic and quite different Greek, whose only near relative in historic times was the dialect of Cyprus. We infer that throughout this area there had once been spoken a Greek ancestral to Arcadian and Cypriote, the language, as Michael Ventris thought, of the Mycenaean world; a speech surviving only in Arcadia, cut off from the sea by the Dorian invaders, and in distant Cyprus, which the invasion did not reach. A further inference is that the invasion or invasions were not the work of mere savages in search of pasture, but of organized war-bands which made deliberately for the south in search of palaces to plunder.

Ill. 4

This point is of some importance. The Greeks at the dawn of their recorded history, in the eighth century, were not in any strict sense primitive. All, even the Dorian late-comers, had been to some extent affected by the Bronze Age civilization; even they had been, in the course of their migrations to new homes, to some extent *detribalized*. It may not have been for anyone's immediate good; but it helps to account for the readiness with which, in the following centuries and under the stimulus of new economic conditions, they adopted and invented new ways. Also the Bronze Age, though the traditions of the Greeks show that they remembered little about its civilization, had left a legacy; a legacy of *techniques*. Writing and palace art had perished, but in the mundane matters of mixed farming, building, carpentry and boat-building, spinning and weaving, metallurgy and the potters' craft, the Greeks of the Geometric period did not begin again where Minoan Crete had begun, but where Mycenae left off.

Homer

Most fruitful of all these legacies was that of the bardic poetry inherited by Homer. As 'hill-billies' in the Appalachian Mountains preserved British songs and ballads, often better remembered than they were in the homeland, so did the descendants of a displaced Greek population in Ionia preserve narrative poems of a Heroic Age, when Mycenae and Pylos had been the homes of kings, and when their ancestors had sacked Troy – and returned to Greece afterwards. The map represented by Homer's list of the contingents at Troy reproduces, indeed, the old Mycenaean world very closely. This is the most concrete evidence that Ionian poets in the eighth century had a well-preserved tradition about that age, five hundred years earlier. They sang the tales of Mycenaean heroes; never, it seems, stories of their own less glorious times, though the daily life described in the poems does combine Mycenaean features with others that appear later and anachronistic. But the two great poems

Ill. 7

4 The first home of Greek civilization was on *both* sides of the Aegean, though the Greeks themselves, when they spoke of Hellas, usually meant the peninsula. The map shows also how that first home was in the south and central Aegean, already that of the Bronze Age civilization; the northern islands and coasts were occupied in the age of colonization

that descended to Classical Greece and to ourselves, the *Iliad* or Tale of Ilios (Troy town) and the *Odyssey*, on the Return of Odysseus, bear the marks not of mere tradition, but of artistic composition by a poetic genius. The name Homeros ('hostage'), though rare, is not unknown in historic Greece; babies were sometimes named after their fathers' condition at the time (like Telemachus, 'fighter afar'). The *Iliad*, of the length of a modern novel, is not a mere chronicle poem; it has a plot, plunging, as the Roman Horace says, at once *in medias res*. Its main action all takes place in a few days, and when traditional material, such as the List of Contingents, is used, it is sometimes

5 This impressive fifth-century Athenian figure of a Rhapsode ('stitcher of songs'), declaiming most probably from the 'Homer' that we still have, illustrates the means by which this aristocratic, originally Ionian, poetry became the common possession of the whole Greek people. Pisistratus as ruler of Athens is said to have organized and systematized the recitations of the great poems at the chief festival of the city's goddess, the Panathenaea; and it may well be that the text of the poems we still read, a text which, in its main lines, was certainly 'fixed' within classical times, is in essence an 'official' text preserved in writing at Athens. The scholars of Alexandria (p. 126) do not seem to have found much to dispute about except minor details

easy to see the 'join', where the poet has adapted it for its new position.

The importance of Homer, and of the poetry and stories that he perfected and transmitted, was enormous. *Ill. 5* He set, for one thing, an unsurpassably high standard of sheer poetic competence. There is nothing primitive about Homer. But even more important than his technique was the influence of his subject-matter. Homer gave to Greece the idea of the Hero, and the Classical conception of the gods. Neither of these is primitive in any sense of the word; but both seem to be (as we may also see by comparison with the Near East, where written history goes back further) highly characteristic of the late Bronze Age, the Age of the Heroes *par excellence*. The Hero is not a tribesman. Either he is a king, owing responsibility to no man, or, if he is a king's henchman, he is quite often an exile from his own country, like *Ill. 6* Achilles' friends Patroclus and Phoenix in the *Iliad*. He is

6, 7 In the seventh century, along with animals and monsters, groups of fighting warriors become a feature of Orientalizing art (pp. 53ff.). Then, a new departure, some artists take to writing in names – names from Homer. So, the group on the famous Rhodian plate, *below*, becomes an illustration to the seventeenth book of the *Iliad*: Menelaus has killed the Trojan Euphorbus but is driven back from his body by Hector. In the Athenian tondo painting, *right*, Achilles renders first aid to Patroclus. It appears that he will have to think again when he comes to tie the ends of the bandage!

above all things an individual, and his supreme motive is the promotion of his own honour and glory. It is the love of honour, *tò philótimon*, as later Greeks were to call it (and still do), the sense of what is due to one even more than from one, that leads Achilles, smarting under an affront from his overlord Agamemnon, to withdraw from the fighting, and sets in motion the main action of the *Iliad*. Homer seems to regard him as wrong (though he never judges) only when he rejects an apology and reasonable amends. He pays dearly for it when his friend Patroclus is killed; and then, with his Wrath (the first and key word of the whole poem) swallowed up in a wrath more bitter, he goes out to slay the slayer, Hector, though his goddess-mother has warned him that if he does, his own fate is soon to fall.

It was not only average Greeks who regarded Achilles' loyalty and unflinching courage as an example to be followed. In Classical Athens Socrates, on trial for his life, uses him as an example of why he cannot change his ways, even if they bring him into danger and ultimately to his end.

Ill. 8

Odysseus, a veteran of forty, shipwrecked and trying to get home to his wife, was a less glamorous hero; but he embodied none the less a Greek ideal. The resourceful, the enduring, to give him his two chief Homeric epithets, he stood, indeed, for what every man might wish to be, whereas not everyone could hope to be as athletic as Achilles, though he could emulate his courage. Without suggesting that Homer single-handed created the Greek character – for obviously he created or elaborated epic characters such as were admired already – Homer certainly did much to fix later society's ideals of manliness: Greek manliness, with its endurance, heroism, craftiness (in Athenian drama Odysseus is sometimes even underhand, which in Homer he is not), its intense individualism and its often fatal *philótimon* and pride.

8 This Athenian vase from Etruria is one of several which depict Odysseus tied to his mast, so that he might hear the Sirens' song without being tempted to fall into their claws. A Siren falls dead from her perch at the shock. The Sirens were localized off Sorrento

Homer also did much to fix men's conception of the Olympic gods: a Bronze Age conception, in which the divine family resembles that of a Mycenaean High King. They feast, drive out in chariots, have their own smith, Hephaestus, and their own doctor, Paean, later identified with Apollo, who in Homer is different. They also quarrel; and here Homer's conception of divinity was even more fateful for Greek history than his ideals of manliness. It looks indeed as though, perhaps already in the epic tradition that he and his original audience inherited, the stories told of the gods were not only ancient, but beginning to be treated not very seriously.

Father Zeus is henpecked by his wife Hera, and bears her down by threats of physical punishment. Aphrodite, the goddess of love, married to the lame smith Hephaestus, has a liaison with the handsome war-god Ares, but is trapped in the act in a snare set by the injured husband, who invites the other gods to come and laugh at his victims. The stories were not taken too seriously for these gods still to be worshipped throughout classical times; but, being found shocking by serious philosophers, they certainly helped to prevent religion from being a bar to the unprecedented freedom of later Greek thought.

The 'Works and Days' of a Greek Farmer

Daily life at the dawn of history in Greece, about 700, is known to us especially from the poem of Hesiod called the *Works and Days*. Starting as a kind of verse letter of expostulation to his unsatisfactory brother, who had quarrelled with him about the division of their inheritance, this poem branches out into a highly interesting exposition of sound mixed farming, on a subsistence basis, but with disposal of surpluses by barter, sometimes involving a boat voyage. Hesiod is not a poor man; he has a yoke of oxen, a cart and an iron-shod plough, and can employ a hired man seasonally; but he is definitely of the people, and grumbles about the 'gift-devouring kings' (local chieftains), to whom his brother had resorted, as to a court, for the satisfaction of his claims. Most interesting is the fact that he is not afraid to grumble so, and that his poem survived. His culture includes some astronomical lore, important for getting farm operations started in good time, but he attaches equal importance to observing lucky and unlucky days of the month; he issues warnings against wasting time, against cutting one's nails on a holy-day (an early appearance of the world-wide superstition about nail-parings), and against letting a boy sit on a tombstone, lest it cause sterility. But he is no

Ill. 9

9 This early bronze, perhaps a votive offering, shows the general shape, or one of the shapes, of the simple plough in use in the world of Hesiod. The ox-team appears to have got out of hand; but this is probably only a rendering of the action of turning

'primitive peasant'. He uses the epic metre and dialect of Homer. His father was not even a native of Boeotia, where he settled, but a 'retro-migrant' from Cyme in the Asian Aeolis. There he had found seafaring an unsatisfactory career, and returned to the old country to take up a farm, in a valley-head, alternately draughty and sun-baked, under Mount Helicon. Hesiod heartily approves of competition between craftsmen (potter and potter, bard and bard), and a reward that he holds out for good farming is 'that you may buy another man's farm, and not he yours'. Nothing could be less primitive than this fact, that in Hesiod's world *land* could be bought and sold. It is the economic basis of *individualism*.

The product of Hesiodic farming is, above all else, grain; wheat if possible, oats, spelt or barley; many crops were mixed. To this day in a Greek village, bread is the 'staff of life' to an extent far greater than in the richer west. Greeks had horned cattle, and bred oxen for the plough; also pigs, goats and sheep; it was while he was keeping his father's sheep on Helicon, Hesiod himself tells us, that the Spirits of Song, the Muses, first spoke to

Ill. 13

10 The olive, Athena's gift, always had its place on Athenian coinage. While the obverse (*cf. Ill. 91*) shows the warrior-goddess in her Classical form, the reverse bears the olive spray and her sacred bird, the owl. Athena's 'perpetual epithet' in Homer is *glaukōpis*, which, though politely translated 'grey-eyed', may literally be rendered as 'owl-faced'. Epithet and emblem perhaps come down from an age when the uncanniness and supposed wisdom of the night-bird were thought to embody a divine power

him; in mythological language, this is no doubt quite true. But no Greek community had enough grazing-land to provide a regular meat diet for most people. Protein (a concept not then known to science) was provided by cheese, fish near the coasts, and above all by the indispensable olive and its oil.

Ill. 10

Ill. 16

The olive tree, the gift of the goddess Athena to her own city, as Athenians proudly claimed, is one of the economic bases of Greek society. It will root and grow even in relatively stony soil. The trees have to be planted in open order, so that corn can be (as in fact it is) grown between them. Trees are valuable property, and can be bought and sold, left by will or given as dowry, independently of the soil they stand in; but the corn harvest (in May) is over long before the olives ripen in autumn, so that lawful access across A's land to X's trees causes no difficulty. The olive is also slow-growing; a tree only begins to be really profitable after about thirty years, and is at its best after fifty. Hence the 'ravaging of the land' that plays so great a part in recorded Greek military history. To trample, burn or (it was done) reap and take home a weaker neighbour's corn hurt him for a season (the records of sieges show that cities usually had a full year's reserves); but to cut down his olives impoverished him for a generation, and would usually compel him, if the invader seemed likely to persist in the hard work involved, to submit to his demands or come out from the city in desperation and fight.

This in turn, it may here be pointed out, is why Classical Greek warfare evolved, as its chief arm, the

11 This famous painting on the inside of a *kylix* (a shallow, stemmed cup; our word 'chalice') by the great artist Exekias, about 540 BC, shows Dionysus in, and indeed having taken total possession of, a ship; a warship or pirate ship, as is shown by the ram. The scene refers, in fact, to the Homeric Hymn to Dionysus, in which the god, walking on the shore in the likeness of a youth, was seized by kidnappers; but, changing into the shape of a lion, he chased them into the sea, where they were turned into dolphins, while the vine of the god sprang up round the ship's mast

12 The new hoplite tactics are shown (*c.* 650–640 BC) in the exquisite drawing of the 'Chigi' vase, found at Veii – a Protocorinthian export to Etruria. Two ranks of armoured men with emblazoned shields advance upon each other with measured tread, keeping step, while on the left a boy piper plays to give the time

Ill. 12

phalanx of heavily armoured spearmen, which could only operate on level ground. Most of Greece is mountainous; but it was the flat, alluvial plains between the hills that were the vital terrain.

Greece also had peas and beans (but not, of course, that valuable New World crop, the potato); onions and garlic for seasoning; and for fruit, apples, pears, quinces, pomegranates, figs, but above all, the vine. Wine was the great giver of joy, and, men said, led to true speaking; and the vintage festival was the year's greatest jollification.

Ill. 11

Demeter (perhaps meaning Mother Earth) and Dionysus, the givers of the Bread and the Wine, little mentioned in the aristocratic poetry of Homer, were the farmers' chief gods, coming into prominence when the farmers gained political influence. In later times the human names based on theirs, Demetrius and Dionysius, became the favourite names in all the extensive Greek repertoire, and passed by way of early saints into the Christian repertoire too. The

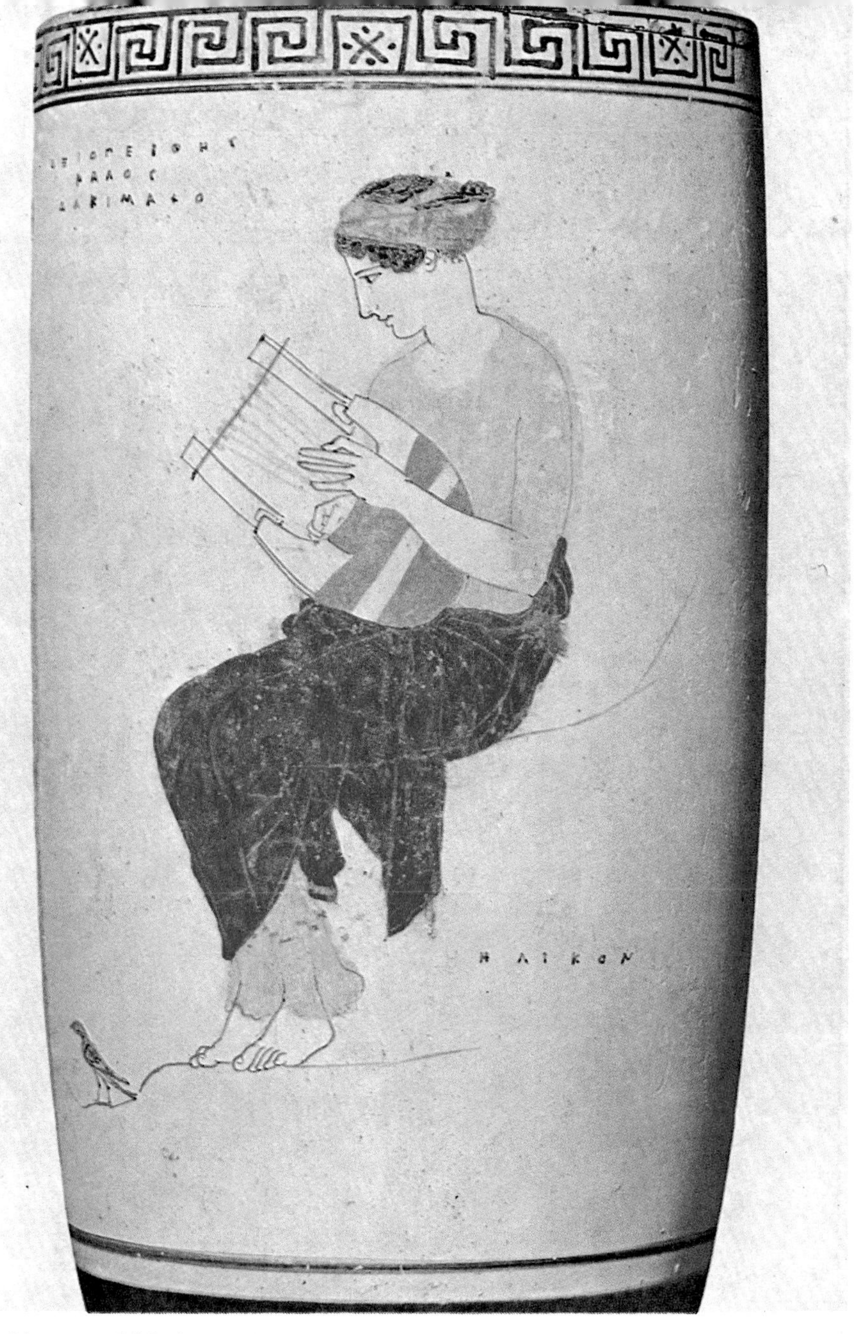

13 A white-ground *lekythos* or oil-flask, a type of vase much used in classical Athens for offerings at tombs, shows a seated woman playing a lyre. But she is no mortal woman. The rising ground on which she sits is clearly labelled, HELIKON. This designates her as one of the Muses, 'who once taught Hesiod' on their holy mountain

◁ 14 This sixth-century Attic amphora gives us our best illustration of that most important operation, the olive-harvest. Men on the ground and a boy up the tree that is being 'harvested' knock down the berries with sticks – contrary, it must be said, to the strictest 'councils of perfection', which would have them individually gathered (if one could reach them). The trees are summarily and conventionally rendered; the interest is centred on the human figures

15 French archaeologists excavating at Argos in recent years discovered the earliest known panoply of hoplite armour (before 700?), and one of the finest and best preserved from any period. The moulding of the corselet, at this early date, is striking. The conical helmet resembles some Assyrian examples, and probably reflects eastern influence. Its high metal crest is meant to carry the typical Greek horsehair plume, regularly shown in the vase-paintings – a style of plume which descends, through Syrian intermediaries, from one shown on the heads of Egyptian chariot-horses. It appears that when the Greek gentleman joined the ranks of the infantry in battle, he hoped still to daunt his opponent with the evidence of his knightly rank

olive harvest, a long, laborious business late in the year, in which every berry had to be picked separately (knocking them down, though done, was wasteful), led to no such junketing. But when it was all done successfully, Greeks like Israelites had 'gladness in their hearts in the day when their corn and wine and oil increased'. *Ill. 14*

Hesiod gives a unique glimpse of the life of a working farmer in the Early Iron Age; but the tone of society was still set by local aristocracies, those chieftains whom he disliked and mistrusted: members of the oldest-established families, who held with family tenacity the best land in each of the fertile but limited plains between the Greek mountains. These were the people who could best afford hired men and slaves, often originally prisoners of war, to do the heavy work, and female slaves for housework,

16, 17 This typical Aegean landscape, *above*, the olives and the sea – the whole background of Greek life at a glance – is in fact on the north coast of Crete, at Mallia, famous for its Minoan palace. *Below*, Olympia, on the rainier west side of Greece, remains a green and pleasant place, though the Aleppo pines are a species introduced recently

18, 19 Delos, the 'birthplace of Apollo', $3\frac{1}{2}$ miles long and less than 2 miles in area, perhaps owed its fame precisely to the fact that, being so small, it was not even a makeweight in political scales. It was *neutral*. Most of the buildings to be seen there are of Roman date: but the famous lions, no less impressive for being so deeply weathered, date from classical Greek times

20 Even Greek artists were not born with a faculty of accurate observation; they learned it, through centuries. On this large amphora, a prize at the Panathenaic Games, the runners have left arm and left leg forward *together*, a position as impossible as the 'flying gallop' of old English sporting prints

including the endless spinning and weaving; or to buy purple cloth or trinkets from Phoenician traders. They could afford the expensive bronze armour, and a horse or, in the earlier days, a chariot, to carry them swiftly and untired over the plain to repel a border raid. Their houses were inside the compact, walled 'city' which grew up in a handy position near every good piece of plain-land; so their wealth, unlike the possessions of outlying farmers, was not exposed to plunder. They could best afford time to listen to travelling bards with tales of the ancient heroes, or to pedlars' or the same bards' accounts of their journeys and of foreign parts; or to travel themselves to festivals, at Delphi in central Greece or Olympia in the Peloponnese, or to Apollo's sacred islet of Delos, a great centre of the Ionian world, where there were athletic sports and the most elaborate bardic recitations; among them, especially at Delos, those from Homer.

Ill. 15

Ills 21, 22

Ills 18, 19

Most famous of all such festivals was the four-yearly athletic meeting at Olympia. Here, in the fertile and well-watered western lowland called by Athenians Hollow Elis, but in the local dialect Walis, the Vale, invaders, not Doric but akin to the Dorians, had established a sanctuary of the Father-God, whom their ancestors in Thessaly had associated with Mount Olympus. There had already been there a sanctuary of the Mother-Goddess of the older folk, who, as Hera, the wife of Zeus, kept her place and temple; and perhaps already in the Bronze Age she had been worshipped by girls with competition in a foot-race; for the length of the course for the girls' race, which still existed, much shrunken in glory, in historic times, was exactly one side of the sacred Grove, the *Altis*. Here – it is not clear why especially here – athletes assembled from all the western Peloponnese; presently also from Sparta and the new western colonies; then from all the Greek world. Other events were added: boxing, wrestling, long-jump, discus, javelin, and long distance running.

Ill. 17

Ill. 21

Ill. 20

21 Mount Olympus, the 'home of the gods'. Foundations of an ancient altar have recently been reported found on the 'Crown of Zeus' (the modern name of one of the highest of these towers) during excavations for a meteorological station

22 The pillars that we see are of a temple built after the earthquake of 373 BC. The substructure is older; but it is the scenery, on a shelf of Mount Parnassus, that makes Delphi, still as in early Greek times, one of the most 'numinous' of Greek sites

To be an Olympic victor was the highest glory known to early historic Greek society; so much so as to call forth from intellectuals some acid remarks about athleticism. Because the four-yearly meeting was an 'international' event, it was found more convenient than (say) the lists of annual magistrates of even the most important cities, as a means of dating historic events. Thucydides, in the fifth century, is the first historian known to us to do this. In his time a learned man of Elis, named Hippias, studied the inscriptions on victory monuments and other records of Olympia, set the names in what he regarded as a probable order, and found that there were enough, allowing one foot-race every four years, to extend back to 776 BC, in terms of our era. This has ever since been reckoned as marking the beginning of the Greek historic era; though whether 'historic' is strictly the right word, is another question.

CHAPTER TWO

Trade and Colonies

'Phoenician Marks': Birth of the Greek Alphabet

The widespread transmission (though not necessarily the invention) of Homer's great artistic epics may have been rendered possible by the recent introduction of the 'Phoenician marks', as Greeks called them, that is the letters of our alphabet, with their Semitic names (alpha = *aleph*, 'ox', originally an ox-head, thus ; it was the Greeks, who, knowing nothing of the meaning, thought it would look much better 'standing up'; beta = the familiar *beth* of Bethel, Bethlehem, meaning 'house', and in the east was originally written something like . The twenty-four letters, some of them switched by the Greeks from representing unneeded Semitic sounds to provide the chief Greek vowel-sounds, represented the best of several simplified writing systems recently developed in the commercial world of the Levant, in the effort to produce, for businessmen, something better than the old syllabaries, which required the services of a professional scribe. Another, much inferior, was the thirty-three letter syllabary of Cyprus, formed by selecting (quite arbitrarily) from the two hundred-odd signs of Minoan Linear B. That Greeks became aware of a need for writing was a sign that communications were becoming more important again, beyond the limits of the parish

23 These letters on a baked clay loom-weight found in the American excavation of the Market Place of ancient Athens, are among the oldest specimens of alphabetic writing that we have from Greece

or the home glen; but in Greece they were used not only for business but for preserving poetry.

Ill. 23

The earliest specimens of Greek alphabetic writing in the new script that we have belong probably to the lifetimes of Homer and Hesiod, and are on fragments of Geometric painted pottery, found near Athens. That is why the prehistoric period in Greece ends at this point.

The cities prospered; they tamed local hillmen; they formed local leagues, as in Boeotia, Phocis and Ionia, or the more powerful established their supremacy over lesser settlements, as did Argos and Sparta; and as security increased, in most places the rich families, the *aristoi* or 'best people' as they called themselves, reduced the powers of the city king who had been essential as a war-leader in the bad times, and took to directing the affairs of the city through annually elected Regents or Presidents. A 'king', sometimes of the old royal family, sometimes, as at Athens, annually elected, often continued to supervise the chief sacrifices; it was safest to give the gods what they were accustomed to. Sometimes the right to elect and to be elected head of state was confined to a clan or group of clans descended from the old kings; sometimes, as at Cyme, it was soon extended to every man who could afford armour and a war-horse. Dandified and sophisticated, the *aristoi* everywhere greatly despised the outlying farmers and hill shepherds, with their skin coats and dirty feet, who bore themselves meekly when they had occasion to come into town. The very idea that such people might have political rights lay still in the future.

The Merchant-Colonists Look West

By about 750 BC, two factors were preparing the revolution which was to transform the Greek world. First, in many regions the available, cultivable land was filling up; the more so, since the great families engrossed what the poor resentfully considered an unfair share of it, and that the best. The tradition never died among the Greek poor that in the Good Old Days some founder-king had divided the city's land fairly, and that, since the division had become very unequal, a *new division* was due. The phrase was to become a revolutionary slogan. To avert the reality became the great political object of aristocratic governments. Otherwise, the only alternatives for the poor, as they multiplied, were greater poverty, or infanticide, which was practised, though Greek mothers resisted it as passionately as any others would, or to conquer a neighbour's land, as Sparta before 700 conquered the lower-lying plain of Messenia; an event which was to be fateful for the whole of Classical Greek history.

A way out (literally) seems to have been revealed by merchants; not Hesiodic farmer-traders, but long-distance seafarers, who made a living out of the fact that, in a world still largely bronze-using not only Greece but the great kingdoms of the east had an insatiable desire for the rare metal, tin. Midas, King of Phrygia, a great figure (Midas of the golden touch, round whose name folk-tales cluster), fought the Assyrians on his eastern frontier, went into alliance with Agamemnon, King of Cyme and dedicated a throne at Delphi; and a merchant

Ill. 24

24 On this ivory relief from the sanctuary of Artemis Orthia at Sparta, a warship prepares to leave harbour under sail. Two sailors are setting the sail, while another fishes from the prow and a fourth crouches on the ram. The figures to the left have been interpreted as Paris leading Helen on board, but are better taken as the captain taking leave of his wife. Letters on the hull dedicate the plaque to the goddess – *ex voto*, after safe return?

of Cyme, Midacritus ('Approved of Midas') was said first to have brought tin from a 'Tin Island' somewhere in the unknown west. It looks like a deliberate effort to establish a metal-trade from Asia Minor, in competition with the Phoenicians, who had already reached Spain along the coast of Africa. This is the context of the epoch-making event, the foundation of the first Greek colony in the west (archaeology confirms a date soon after 750 BC), by Cyme together with Chalcis, the 'bronze-town' in Euboea, famous for its metal-work; it too was called Cyme (in Greek, Küme), a name more famous in its Latin dress: the Cumae of Virgil.

Ill. 25

Cumae, planted far afield on the Bay of Naples, looks like a trading outpost, like its Phoenician contemporary, Carthage ('New Town') in Tunisia; but it was soon followed by a whole series of new ventures, which went less far and seized the best coastal land (not always the best harbours) from weak native populations in eastern Sicily and South Italy. Chalcis, probably recruiting land-hungry men also from other cities, such as Naxos, founded a new Naxos, near Taormina, the first Greek

25 The more spacious world, to which western colonization introduced the Greeks at the beginning of their great expansive period. Few of the colonies (only Taranto, Syracuse, Cumae and on a smaller scale Zancle, the later Messina) had really good harbours; but this mattered the less since Greek ships were regularly drawn up on beaches. The wealth and large populations of the colonies came from their land; Leontini in Sicily is actually inland; though there was also probably some middleman trade across the 'toe' of Italy. Powerful Sybaris and Croton had daughter-colonies on the west coast, and traders from Sybaris could probably even use the valley routes to her more distant colony of Poseidonia (Paestum)

26 At Syracuse, Thucydides tells us, Archias of Corinth 'drove the Sikels [native Sicilians] first from the Island' which occupies nearly the whole of this aerial photograph. Expansion across the narrow, tidal inlet, and indeed over the whole south-east corner of Sicily, soon followed; but the Island, now closely built-up, retained strategic significance; Syracusan tyrants used it as a citadel

town in Sicily, and a base for the conquest of more roomy sites further south (Catana, Leontini); she also founded Rhegium (Reggio in Calabria), and reduced to order an unofficial pirate settlement of Greeks on the Straits, now Messina.

Corinth, already with an eye for harbours, founded Syracuse and colonized Kerkyra (Corfu island), a useful half-way house. The Achaeans of the northern Peloponnese, who were not traders but lacked land at home, got the best agricultural sites of all, at Sybaris, Croton and Metapontum in South Italy; Sparta, 'reconstructing' after the conquest of Messenia, planted out 'war-babies' and other dissatisfied elements at Taras (Taranto); Rhodians of Lindos and Cretans, already accustomed to trade with the Levant, but unable to colonize there in face of the Assyrian Empire, came to Gela on the south coast of Sicily. All this is said to have been done between 735 and 690 BC (the real dates are perhaps a little later).

27 The badge on coins of Metapontum illustrates the importance of the wheatfields of Magna Graecia

28 The Syracusan Temple of Athena stood on the highest point of the Island. Taken over as a Christian church in the fourth century AD, its colonnades are now incorporated in medieval and baroque masonry, though the lines of the Greek temple can still be made out, and its fine Doric columns remain visible. They are monolithic, in the early Greek manner, later replaced, as in the Parthenon, by the practice of building columns with carefully fitted 'drums'. This temple, which no doubt itself occupied the site of an earlier and smaller structure, is assigned by experts to the early fifth century. That is to say that it was built under the tyrants of the House of Deinomenes, and most probably was initiated by the soldier-prince Gelon, as a thank-offering for his crowning mercy, the defeat of Carthaginian invasion in the critical summer of 480 (p. 87)

There was a long pause before the expansion to western Sicily. Then Megara, a small colony near Syracuse – founded when its mother-city, old Megara, was a vassal of Corinth – sent out men to Selinus (Selinunte), after 630, and Gela to Acragas (Agrigento), later famous for its splendid temples, half-way to Selinus, about 580. By this time also the Asian Greek Ionians of Phocaea, a neighbour of Aeolic Cyme, which seems to replace Cyme in the western trade (we do not know why), were colonizing from the Riviera (Nice, Antibes, Monaco) to Spain; Massalia (Marseille), their great success, was only the greatest among many colonies; and their early walls at Ampurias (Emporiae, 'the Trade-posts'), about 520, are the westernmost considerable remains surviving of any Greek city.

Ill. 30

Ill. 29

South Italy became known as Greater Greece, Magna Graecia. In the west, thousands of Greeks enjoyed for the first time the sense that there was land enough and to

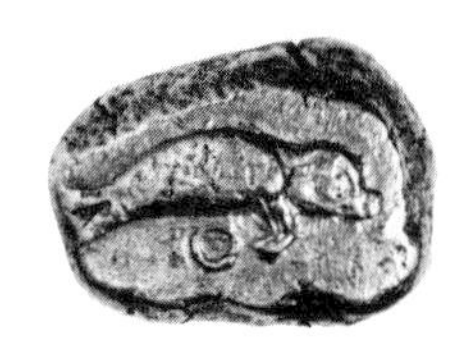

29 Early electrum (mixed gold and silver) coin of Phocaea, with her punning badge: *phoka*=a seal

30 The 'Temple of Concord' at Agrigento, the Greek Akragas, was also used as a Christian church, and, like the 'Theseion' at Athens, owes to this its fine preservation. It is a sophisticated structure (latish fifth century?) embodying refinements probably first worked out at Athens. The name 'Concord' is erroneous; the actual dedication is unknown

spare. On the miniature scale of the Greek world, it was to the old country as America to Europe. Its cities grew larger and richer than any in the old country except Athens in her prime, and made their own contribution to art, literature, philosophy, medicine and engineering.

Ill. 36

Colonization in other areas was important, but all of it together not so important as the west. Cyrene, founded by the Dorian island of Thera (Santorin), and later reinforced from all over the Aegean, alone could compare with such cities as Sybaris. Founded a few miles inland, it exported corn and the medicinal laxative herb silphium (now extinct), founded daughter-cities west-

Ills 31, 32

31 The silphium plant (as is reasonably supposed) on a coin of Cyrene. Cyrene, like Metapontum, uses for its reverse badge a plant important to its economy

ward to Euhesperidae (Benghazi), and long preserved the hereditary monarchy (*c.* 630–450 BC).

Eastward Expansion

Colonization in the North Aegean began later than in the west, surprisingly at first sight; but the large, blond Thracians were a different proposition, as opponents, from the western Sicels. Only perhaps, when Corinth began to monopolize trade with Sicily, did Chalcis and Eretria in Euboea turn to the three-pronged peninsula, later known as Chalcidice, and Megara, now independent of Corinth and on bad terms with her, to the Sea of Marmara, The coast of the Troad and some sites in the Chersonese (Gallipoli Peninsula) had already been occupied by a coastwise spread of settlements from Lesbos and continental Aeolis; Mytilene, largest of the five cities of Lesbos, kept those in the Troad dependent when she could. Megara looked further, and founded two famous cities astride the Bosporus, Chalcedon and, in 629 according to a local historian, Byzantium.

Ill. 36

Ionian traders had already visited the Black Sea coasts; but the great outpouring of colonists thither seems to begin only after events in Asia Minor had cut off the cities there from the hope of expanding by land. The Phrygian kingdom was destroyed about 676 by migrating barbarians, the Cimmerians, driven south by the coming of the eastern horse-archer Scythians, like Goths before the Huns; and its western successor-state, Lydia, with its capital at Sardis only a day's ride from the sea, first drove out the Cimmerians and then pressed Ionia hard, destroying Smyrna about 600 BC and attacking Miletus at the mouth of the Maeander valley. However Gyges (*c.* 678–648), founder of the Lydian military dynasty, while he may have cut short Miletus' territory at home, allowed her to colonize Abydos, on the narrows of the Dardanelles, opposite Sestos; and thereafter Miletus, with

Ill. 80

32 Dorian Cyrene kept up close ties with Sparta, whose port of Gythion lay only two days away, given a fair wind; and it is a sixth-century Laconian artist who gives our most vivid picture of its commercial monarchy. King Arkesilas II (named in writing), wearing an ornate and probably royal head-dress, sits on his folding-stool, supervising the weighing and storing of a commodity, probably wool, for which his land was famous. Below, it is stored in bales in a vault. The monkey, the crane flying past, and the gecko lizard are all African touches

recruits, we may guess, from other cities, directed a remarkable colonizing enterprise; she was said to have founded seventy cities in the Black Sea and its approaches. Among the most important were Sinope, probably *c.* 630, though some Greek computations (which also grossly antedated Cyrene) made it much earlier; Trapezous

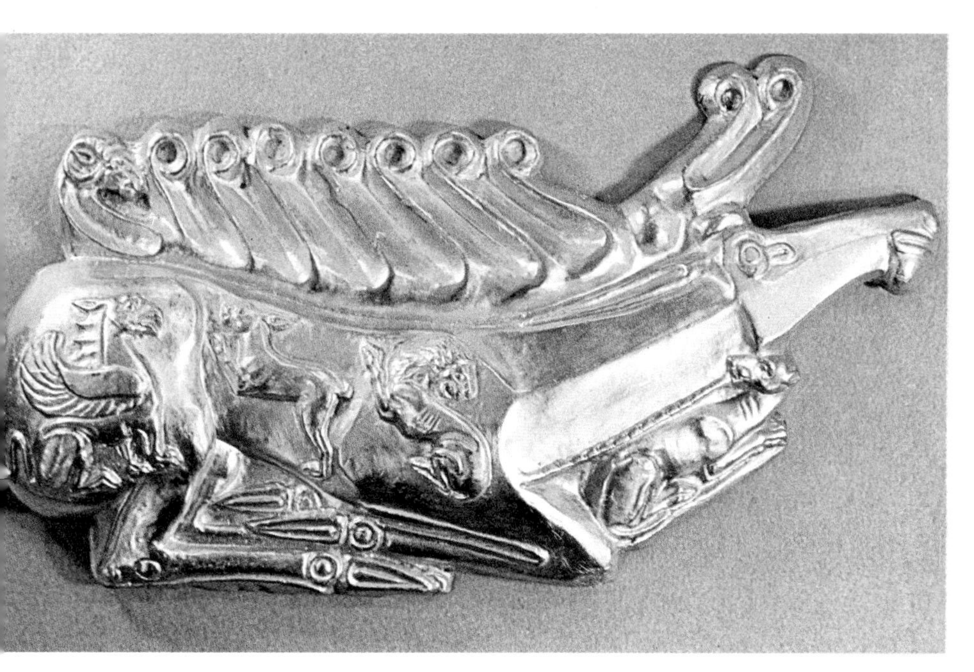

33–35 The wealth which Scythian kings derived from their contacts with the Greeks are shown in the great treasures of gold, silver and electrum from royal tombs in South Russia, the best dating from the fourth century. Among the most thoroughly Greek pieces are those from the tomb at Kul Oba, near Kerch in the Crimea. The fine stag plaque (*above*) clearly imitates the northern Animal Style of art, but it is the work of a Greek artist. The famous electrum vase, *below right*, with scenes of Scythian life, shows in Greek realistic style the Scythian costume. The silver, parcel-gilt vase, *below left*, treats in Greek style animal motifs of oriental origin

(Trebizond), a daughter-colony of Sinope; and Olbia ('Prosperity'), not far from modern Odessa in the Ukraine. Megara also took part in this movement, with several colonies; her largest was Heraclea in Bithynia, which included many settlers from Boeotia.

These Black Sea and northern colonies were of enormous importance to Classical Greece, as sources of foodstuffs and raw materials: grain, fish, timber, leather from Scythia, iron, gold and other minerals from south of the Caucasus, and slaves; but in culture, unlike those of the west, they seem to have remained 'colonial'. In literature and art they followed the mother country; and when, in later days, they produced famous intellectuals, such as Aristotle from Chalcidice, or Diogenes (of the Tub) from Sinope, they not only went to study in the old country, but tended to stay there. Among Greek exports some magnificent Late Classical gold vessels, found in the burial-mounds of Scythian chiefs, vividly portray Scythian costume and life.

Ills 33–35

In the Levant, Woolley's excavations at Al-Mina have shown that a Greek trading colony was established before 700 on the coast of North Syria; its name was probably Posidium. But, like Greek ventures into Cilicia, it was unable to make good its hold permanently against Assyrian and Phoenician hostility. The easternmost typical Greek colony here (not counting the Mycenaean foundations in Cyprus) was Rhodian Phaselis in Lycia. Yet the Levant trade (Greek metals, wine, pottery and other manufactures against spices, purple, oriental metal-work, ivory and apes and engraved ostrich-eggs – peacocks only later) remained important, despite intermittent warfare. Its impact on the newly expanding culture of Greece was tremendous, as may be seen in the Orientalizing movements in Greek art.

Particularly stimulating to Greek intelligence was the contact with Egypt, where thousands of Greeks went,

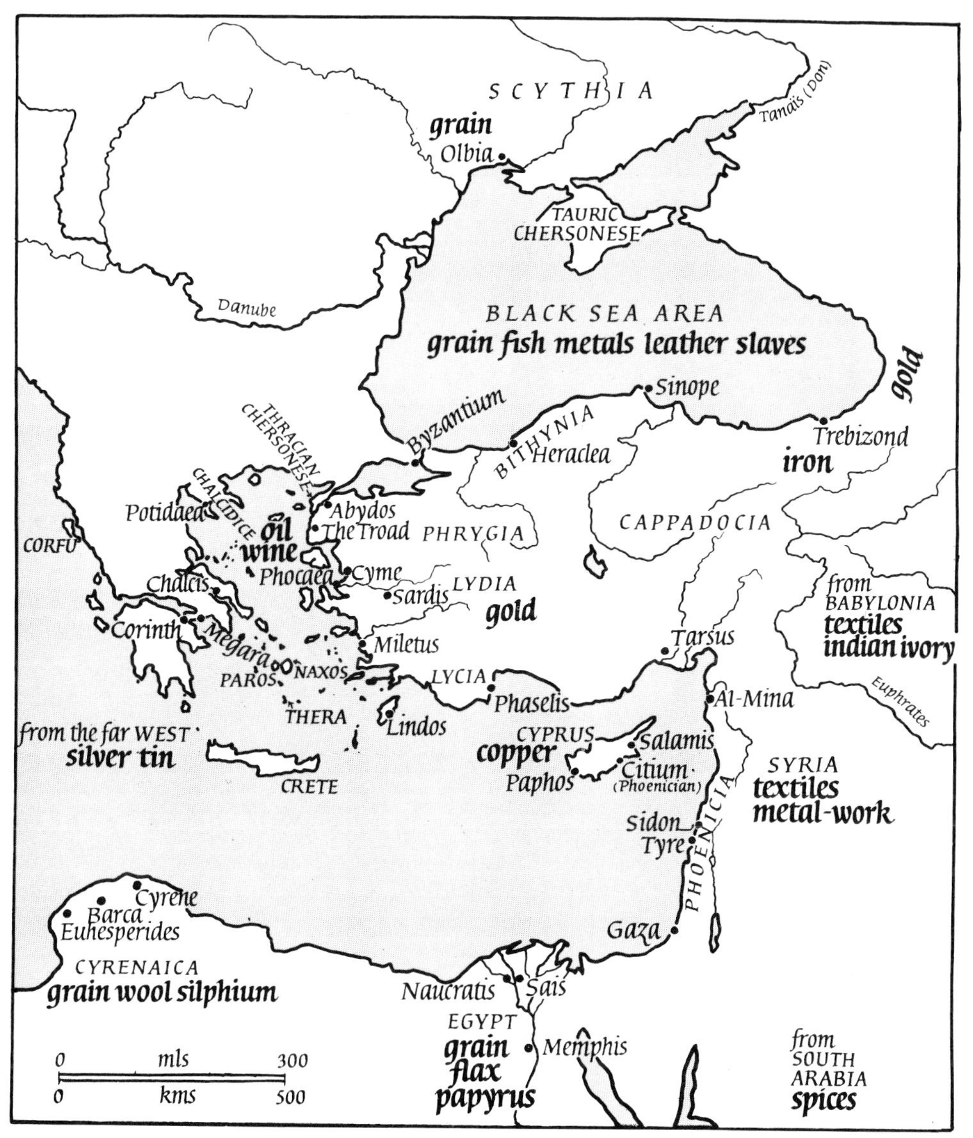

36 This map, of an area rarely illustrated as one, shows among other things how large was this eastern world compared to the Aegean. Greeks naturally acquired much local knowledge of weather and currents. The summer north wind (the 'annual wind', as they called it) was useful in bringing home laden ships from the Black Sea; and Cretan sea-raiders in the *Odyssey* (xiv) reach Egypt in four days 'without rowing'. But the same wind could create great difficulties for ships north-bound; one might be stuck for weeks before being able to round Malea, the south-east cape of the Peloponnese; and the strong south-westward current of the Dardanelles posed a particularly formidable problem

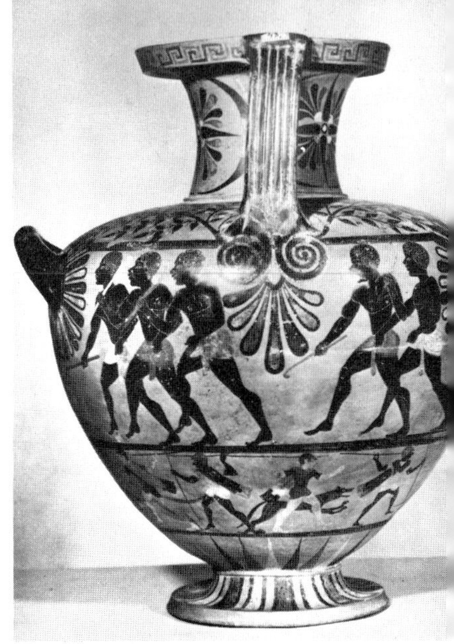

37, 38 The legend of the wicked King Busiris of Egypt is purely Greek; the name is really that of a place, 'Sanctuary of Osiris'. Busiris, the legend said, was promised by a foreign prophet deliverance from famine if he sacrificed a foreigner every year. Busiris sacrificed the prophet, and continued the process with excellent results until Heracles, on one of his quests, entered the country and they tried to sacrifice him. Heracles broke loose at the altar and made havoc of the Egyptians. The story was very popular; dramatized by Ephicharmus of Syracuse (*c.* 490?), and repeatedly illustrated by vase painters, never better than on this Ionian water-vessel from Caere in Etruria

'both to trade' says Herodotus 'and to see the country', and many of them to serve in the armies of the Twenty-Sixth Dynasty. Some of them carved their names on a leg of one of Ramesses II's colossi at Abu Simbel. The extraordinary character of the country, 'gift of the Nile' (Herodotus again) stimulated geological speculations; its wholly alien culture opened Greek eyes to the fact that customs were not necessarily as they were at home; its vast antiquity opened new vistas of time; but some contempt for mere 'natives' is shown on the famous Busiris Vase, where Herakles makes havoc of the Egyptians who tried to sacrifice him, while on the back the black police arrive too late. These successful foreigners were not popular in Egypt, and presently there was an anti-foreign movement; but its leader Amasis, who

Ill. 40
Ills 39, 41
Ills 37, 38

39–41 'When King Psammatichos came to Elephantina, this wrote they, who sailed with Psammatichos the son of Theokles, and came above Kerkis, as far as the river let them. And Potasimto led the foreigners, and Amasis the Egyptians. And Archon, son of Amoibichos, and Axe, son of Nobody, wrote me.' Seldom has a piece of vandalism left results that have come to be so historic and romantic as when Greek mercenaries, on the way back from an expedition up the Nile, carved this text (shown below) and several of their names on a leg of one of Ramesses II's colossi at Abu Simbel. The historic site is shown above, as it was before its removal from the dangers of inundation beneath the waters of the High Dam. *Right*, unfinished relief of a hoplite, perhaps one of these same mercenaries, from the Greek 'international settlement' at Naucratis

42 'Ekstratos dedicated me to Aphrodite': on this Chian bowl from Naucratis, as at Abu Simbel, the inscribed object is made to 'speak'. The Naucratite sanctuary of the goddess of love was great and wealthy, as its large numbers of dedications show; the 'love', not unpredictably in an international seaport, was largely mercenary. The *hetairai* ('girl-companions') of Naucratis were famous; Herodotus praises their beauty. He also mentions how one of them charmed Charaxus, brother of the poetess Sappho and himself a gentleman trader, who paid her so handsomely that she was able to buy herself out of slavery and go into business on her own account; a transaction on which Sappho commented with sisterly acidity. It is the earliest outside information that we have on Sappho and her family (*cf.* pp. 62 ff.)

Ills 40, 42

reigned as Pharaoh 569–529 BC, permitted the Greeks to continue trading through one port, Naucratis ('Sea-Power'), seized as a fort by Miletus long before. Here Greeks from many cities collaborated in the administration of the city and its temples; it was a unique 'treaty-port', presenting analogies to the Shanghai of recent times.

CHAPTER THREE

The Age of Revolution

In the transition from 'medieval' or Hesiodic to 'modern' or Classical Greece, the period from about 660 to 500 BC is an age of renaissance and revolution. Traders in metal and valuable goods, we saw, had probably pioneered where colonists followed; but colonization itself gave rise to a far more massive trade. Cities had colonized because their peasants needed land on which to grow food; now, the new western colonies, with their good land, could produce a surplus, while on the other hand they wanted the luxury goods, such as the best pottery, metal-work and textiles, which were in short supply under 'frontier' conditions. Few new colonies were planted after about 500, partly because the best sites were occupied, and because in the west the Phoenicians, led by Carthage, went into alliance with native peoples to hold back the Greeks; but also because it was now possible to import food in exchange for manufactures (also oil and wine to the Black Sea), instead of exporting men.

Orientalizing Art

The art of the east had been known to Greeks since the mid-eighth century, through Al-Mina, through Phoenician traders like those mentioned in the *Odyssey*, who

43–45 Oriental floral ornament and its adaptation in Greece. The ivory plaque from Nimrud in Assyria (no doubt from the decoration of palace furniture), *below right*, shows one type of Eastern original; but even more influential was the Egyptian design of lotus-buds and flowers, stylized ultimately into the classical 'egg and dart' pattern. On the capital from Naucratis, *below left*, it is still close to the original Egyptian form. On the Ionic frieze from Delphi, *above*, while the flowers are naturalistic, the palmettes are already classical in style

46 The 'Bokkhoris' vase, from Tarquinia, so-called because it bears the name of that Pharaoh in hieroglyphics, encircled by the customary *cartouche*, whether genuine Egyptian or a Phoenician imitation, is a vulgarly expensive piece of 'trade-goods'. It is clearly important for dating the opening-up of the trade routes; but it must be remembered that, while Bokkhoris reigned *c.* 718–712 (later Greek chronology puts him much too early), his name might have been copied later for commercial purposes

often peddled a somewhat vulgarized and commercial Egypto-Syrian amalgam of their own, and through voyages to Egypt as early as the days of the Pharaoh Bokkhoris (718–712); a name that Greeks remembered, while its appearance on a vase in faraway Etruria is a significant piece of dating evidence. Phoenician bronze-work and eastern ivories appear in Geometric contexts in Greece. But it is not till a generation after the great Sicilian colonizing movement that Greeks suddenly throw off the Geometric convention and strike out new lines in what became for a century a strongly Orientalizing art style. The ornamentation of the new pottery reproduces many motifs from oriental textiles, such as we may see on the robes of Assyrian kings in their sculptured reliefs; evidence that textiles were important among luxury imports. Often they became in Greece simply conventional ornaments; the Babylonian Sacred Tree, with its branches connected with ribbons like a

Ill. 46

Ills 49, 51, 52

Ills 47, 48

47 Ivory inlay (again from Nimrud) for a bed-head; a type of furniture possessed also by wealthy Hebrews, and mentioned more than once by the Prophets as a luxury of the greedy rich. Its particular interest in the present context is concentrated in the two outside panels, where the 'tree' ornament repeats again and again the motif of the shoot between the two shorter, outward-curving members: the ancester, through intermediate Greek stages, of the volutes of the classical Ionic pillar-capital

Ills 43–45

Christmas-tree, or the volutes, palmette, and 'egg and dart', destined to a history in Classical architectural ornament down to this day; but that the Greeks knew that it represented a real vegetable is shown, for instance, on a Rhodian vase, where two agreeably lively goats are eating one. The whole movement is the expression of a new mood in the cities, of confidence born of the overseas expansion; a feeling that there is space and food in the world for everyone.

Ill. 50

Individualism burgeons with affluence. Artists begin to sign their works; and in poetry, short personal and occasional pieces, songs, satires, laments and expressions of proverbial wisdom, such as must always have existed, now first begin to be written down and remembered for posterity.

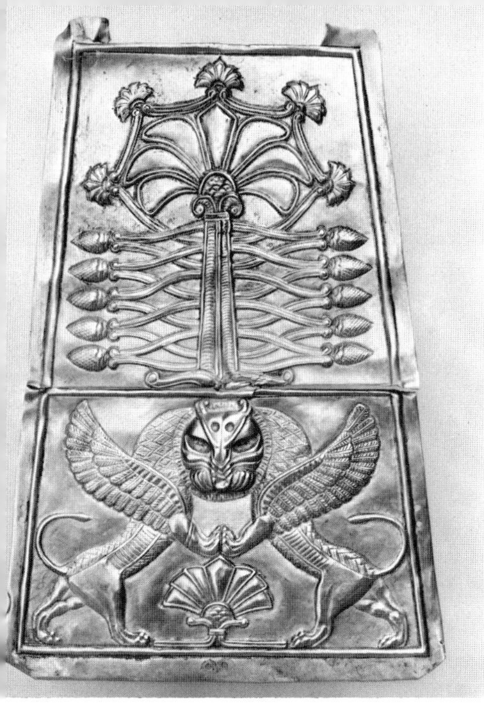

48–50 Oriental and Orientalizing: the gold plaque from Ziweyeh, *above left*, is among eastern prototypes of two subjects taken up in Greece: the Sacred Tree, popular as a motif on Greek vase-handles, and that strange monster, the beast with one head and two bodies (was it originally meant to show opposite side-views of one body?). The latter is imitated, for instance, on the Ripe Corinthian jug, *above right*, of about 600 BC. *Below*, on the small, stemmed bowl from Rhodes (*c.* 625 BC), we have the concrete evidence that seventh-century Greece still thought of the palmette as a palm

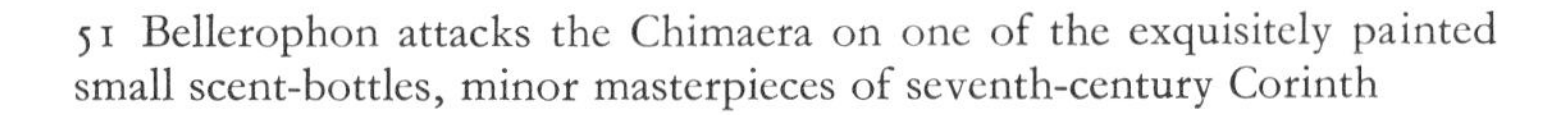
51 Bellerophon attacks the Chimaera on one of the exquisitely painted small scent-bottles, minor masterpieces of seventh-century Corinth

Personal Poetry

The first great name in the 'new' poetry is that of a typical child of his time: Archilochus of Paros, son of a nobleman, but by a slave mother; so, near the aristocracy but not of it; a man with a chip on his shoulder. His poetry is lost, save for fragments (later writers' quotations); but the Classical writers spoke of him in the same breath with Homer. Taking part in a colony led by his father to the northern island of Thasos (where his father no doubt felt that he was doing the decent thing, seeing his bastard planted on a farm of his own); falling in love, jilted, and avenging himself in satires, that were said to have driven the girl and her father to suicide; throwing away his shield in a defeat of gold-mining colonists on the mainland by the Thracians, and writing humorously to a friend that he has saved his life and can soon get another shield; making Thasos too hot to hold him and embarking on a career as a mercenary – regarded as one of the lowest forms of life – he is for ever in trouble and for ever defiant. He writes of war and the sea and wine and women, in anti-romantic, anti-heroic style; and yet his verse can also have a piercing beauty; it was that which made him different. In an age that valued poetry, it appears that Paros (his half-brothers?) welcomed him home in middle age; and in a war with Naxos, the neighbouring island and traditional enemy, he was killed in battle.

Archilochus is the articulate representative of all those thousands of the unprivileged, to whom the new age opened a career. This naturally did not mean that most of them were contented. On the contrary, they became all the less inclined to acquiesce in the government of closed aristocracies, each consisting of a ring of old-established landed families. The aristocracies had themselves organized the great colonizing expeditions, because the best way of keeping their lands at home was to provide for the land-hungry abroad; but they now had to face the

52 This magnificent little Protocorinthian aryballos (*c.* 640 BC), less than two inches high, has thirty-three separate figures, in three zones

challenge, not only of the footloose like Archilochus or of the enterprising new-rich merchants and sea-captains, but even of the home farmers, many of whom, with more elbow-room in the land, were able to rise into the 'armoured' class. In city after city, where the unprivileged could find a leader, the closed circle was broken in favour of a dictatorship, sometimes of a plebeian leader, more often of an ambitious, dissident nobleman or of someone who (like Archilochus) was connected with but excluded from the old ruling class. Cypselus of Corinth, who overthrew the aristocracy there, came of the ruling and formerly royal clan through his mother; but she, because she was lame, had found no husband within the clan and been married off to a non-Dorian farmer. Cypselus rose in the army, and overthrew the government (657, traditionally; probably really later) a few years after it had failed in an attempt to assert overlordship over the colony at Corfu.

Orthagoras of Sicyon, Corinth's neighbour, who about the same time founded a dynasty that lasted a hundred years, is said to have been the son of a cook. His descendant Cleisthenes raised the non-Dorian population, organized in a tribe called the Coast-men, to a status equal or superior to the Dorians, and renamed their tribe 'Rulers'. Such revolutionary despots were called 'tyrants', a word not originally hostile; it is not Greek, nor apparently, as used to be thought, Lydian; but *serens*, the Biblical name of the lords of the Philistines (who had come to Palestine from the Aegean or the nearby Asian coast in the great migrations of about 1200) may perhaps show a common origin.

Corinth, whose fine 'Proto-Corinthian' pottery at this time dominated if it did not monopolize the western markets, is the best-known city of this age. Cypselus ruled it for thirty years, popular except with those whom he had overthrown, and his son Periander for forty-four

Ill. 55
Ills 49, 51, 52

53 To dig a Corinth Canal proved always beyond the means of the ancient world, though the emperor Nero got as far as starting work on one; but Periander did inaugurate a second-best project: a *diolkos* or tramway, on which ships could be hauled on many-wheeled transporters, from sea to sea. Sails were set if the wind was favourable, while going uphill, and cargo was unloaded; so the portage was expensive, but it did save the voyage round Cape Malea, with the possibility of lengthy delays there (*cf. Ill. 36*). It had also a strategic use. Aristotle tells how Periander's warships were active on 'both seas'

years – but by now the 'honeymoon period' was over, and he had to surround himself with guards. He established a slipway, by which ships could be hauled across the Isthmus; he subdued Corfu, and founded other colonies on the north-west coasts of Greece, which, exceptionally among Greek colonies, always remained dependent on the mother-city; and he patronized the Lesbian poet Arion. Money – a Lydian invention, first brought into Europe by the trading island of Aegina about 625 BC (not earlier, as used to be thought) – was first struck at Corinth in his time. But his later years were darkened by family quarrels; his sons died before him – one in a new colony at Potidaea in Chalcidice, one in a chariot accident, one murdered at Corfu – and his successor, a nephew, Psammetichus (named, it is interesting to see,

54 The obverse type of a silver stater of the island of Aegina, with its badge, a turtle

55, 56 These seven sturdy, monolithic pillars of the Temple of Apollo are virtually all that remains above ground of pre-Roman Corinth. Here we face north across the head of the Gulf towards Perachora (far left), where Humfry Payne made his sensational discoveries of Greek orientalizing art. *Right*, the splendid gold bowl, said to come from Olympia, is inscribed on the outside, 'The sons of Cypselus dedicated [this, as spoil] from Heraclea' – probably a small city in north-west Greece

after a Pharaoh of Egypt) was overthrown after three years, traditionally in 581 (the real date may be as much as thirty years later). Corinth then became a bourgeois republic; but, as membership of the governing class seems to have been open to anyone with a moderate property qualification, it was a very different republic from that ruled exclusively by the old royal Bacchiad clan.

Mytilene, Miletus

What the aristocrats themselves thought about all this is revealed, in uninhibited reactionary sentiments, by the great poet Alcaeus of Mytilene, largest of the five cities of Lesbos.

Mytilene was the home of a gifted and artistic community. Its early coins are among the most beautiful in all Greece, and girls of good families from Ionia, it appears, went to learn music and deportment in the houses of ladies of Mytilene, one of whom, famous in her own right, was the poetess Sappho. Sappho is one of the most untranslatable of poets, since there is nothing profound in her thought, and even her imagery, the element in poetry which abides translation, loses much without the golden language. (It may be observed that to learn as much of Sappho's language as many English readers know of Dante's, it is not *essential* to learn first the very different dialects of Homer and Plato.) For the social historian, however, she gives our only glimpse between Homer and Classical Athens of women's life: its high points, worship; weddings (with some heavy jokes); girls at leisure, admiring an army parade or a fleet at sea, or singing to each other while plaiting crowns of flowers; love. Sappho (a married woman with a daughter of her own) loved many of her pupils passionately; she is almost sick with rage when one of them leaves her for a rival teacher, misses them when they leave in the normal course to be married, and writes to them in verse

Ill. 58

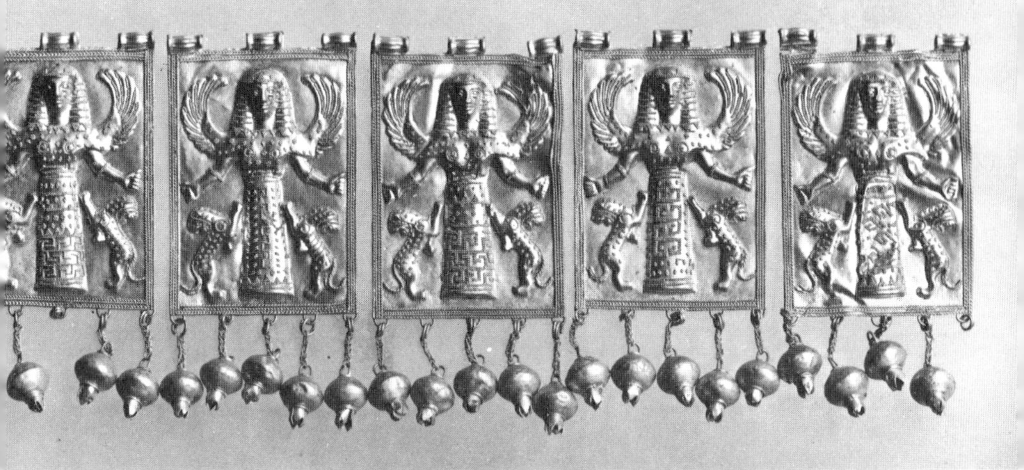

57, 58 *Above*, a gold plaque from Rhodes, with panels showing the Mistress of Beasts, and pomegranate pendents. Though the goddess is Artemis and not Aphrodite, it may be taken to stand for what Sappho's mental picture of a goddess would have been. *Below*, a fifth-century Athenian conception of Alcaeus, in his poetic, not his warlike, character, and Sappho. It might well illustrate lines attributed to him, in a rhythm ingeniously suggesting both his favourite metre and hers: 'Violet-crowned, holy, honey-sweet-smiling Sappho: I wish to speak, but awe restrains me.' Sappho, it is said, replied (in Alcaic metre): 'If your desire was noble or fair, and your tongue not brewing some base thing to say, shame would not be upon your eyes, but you would have spoken of what is right'

afterwards. That Sappho's establishment was a hot-bed of lesbian practices is a piece of scandal we owe chiefly to later Athenian comedy, which at one stage made much use of burlesque literary history for plots. Greek parents were by no means indifferent to the morals of their daughters; and they still sent them to Sappho.

Ill. 58

Alcaeus, many of whose poems are political – he invented the metaphor of the storm-tossed ship of state in one of them – shows us the break-up of the old, aristocratic society. The people grow restive; the nobles try to maintain order with the big stick (literally); a popular leader draws the sword, and blood is shed. More than one 'tyrant' was killed by Alcaeus' friends; but the tide turned when Pittacus, a nobleman who was afterwards counted one of the Seven Sages of early Greece, went over to one such leader's party, and after the latter's death at the hands of the reactionaries was elected dictator ('tyrant' according to Alcaeus) and drove the die-hards out. They, in exile, took service with the kings of the east. A tattered fragment of a poem speaks tantalizingly of Ascalon (in Philistia), of Babylon – whose king at the time was that Nebuchadrezzar, who sacked Jerusalem in 589. Finally they tried again to overthrow Pittacus, who captured them all, and, to their great surprise pardoned them. He then completed his overhaul of the laws and, after ruling for ten years, retired into private life. So Alcaeus, if in 'reduced circumstances', lived to be old.

Not all cities were so well guided. Miletus and Megara, the colonizers of the Black Sea, both, after experience of tyrannies, wasted their strength in bitter civil strife. That at Megara provides the background to the naïve reflections of Theognis, a lesser poet than Alcaeus, but better preserved; his work was favoured as a school-book by Athenian conservatives. Miletus too had her poet, known only from a few quotations, Phocylides, an interesting character. He pleads for moderation: 'a little city on a rock, with order, is better than madness in Nineveh'. Again, 'all virtue is summed up in justice'. Virtue, *aretē*, in Homer is a quality that could be shared by a horse or a sword. What Phocylides is saying is that human virtue is *moral* virtue; it is a landmark in the emergence of Greek moral philosophy. He pleads too that the best road to wealth is 'to cultivate one's field' (Voltaire would have approved); and it was under the landed interest that Miletus was at last given peace by arbitrators from Paros, after a generation of mutual atrocities between parties called the Rich and the Workers in the great port.

Yet it was in this very generation of bitterness and unrest that, in Miletus itself, Greek philosophy and scientific speculation were born. Thales, who was said to have predicted an eclipse in 585 (if so, it may have been a lucky guess); his disciple Anaximander, who propounded a theory of the evolution of man from sea-creatures, perhaps taking a hint from Babylonian mythology; Anaximenes, Anaximander's disciple, who defined his master's primal matter, the Undefined or Unlimited, as 'a mist', *aēr* (later the word for 'air'), by whose condensation liquids and solids are formed; all these three were Milesians. They were followed in Ionia by Pythagoras of Samos, mathematician and mystic, and Xenophanes of Colophon, who like Pythagoras emigrated to the west after the Persian conquest of Lydia and Ionia in 540. Xenophanes made observations on fossils, mocks in his verses at the old stories of quarrelsome and immoral anthropomorphic gods and at Pythagoras' doctrine of the transmigration of human souls into animals, and preaches a bold and intellectual monotheism. But both Pythagoras and he were mocked in turn (in prose, this time) as mere collectors of bits of learning, by the profound Heracleitus of Ephesus, father of the dialectical concept of the unity of opposites, which was to be taken up in turn by Hegel and Marx.

So the very turbulence of Greek society and the inadequacy of its religion were bringing forth giant off-spring; but the instability of the society itself, and the advance of Persia, were meanwhile menacing the whole future of Greek civilization. To the question, how it could be saved, opposite answers were already being propounded by the two states that were to dominate the Classical period, Sparta and Athens.

The Strange Community of Sparta

Ill. 59

Sparta, to judge by her archaeology, was in the seventh century BC an opulent, aristocratic state, her nobles grown rich on the surplus extracted from serfs, the helots, in Laconia, and from the farmers of Messenia, reduced to helot status. Her attempts to expand further led to defeat by Argos; and late in the century the Spartans found themselves fighting for their lives against a desperate Messenian rebellion with support from Arcadia. It was in this war that they were encouraged to persevere by the verses of Sparta's most characteristic poet, Tyrtaeus. It was after this that Sparta became 'Spartan', bringing back into full vigour and further elaborating the 'Laws of Lycurgus' (a mythical figure) including archaic customs, such as the rest of Greece was discarding or had discarded. That these customs now resuscitated were part of the old Dorian tribal heritage is suggested by the fact that the Dorian nobles of Crete, the better to control their own serfs, the *Mnoïtes* (Minoans?) had taken similar steps rather earlier. This gave rise to a theory, mentioned by Herodotus, that Lycurgus introduced his laws from Crete. In both areas, the laws included restrictions on individualism and family life; the men, for instance, took their meals in military messes. The sequel, in both areas, was that local art, after showing early promise, wilted and died – though not at once. The huge Vix Crater, a gift from traders of Marseille to some

Ills 60, 61

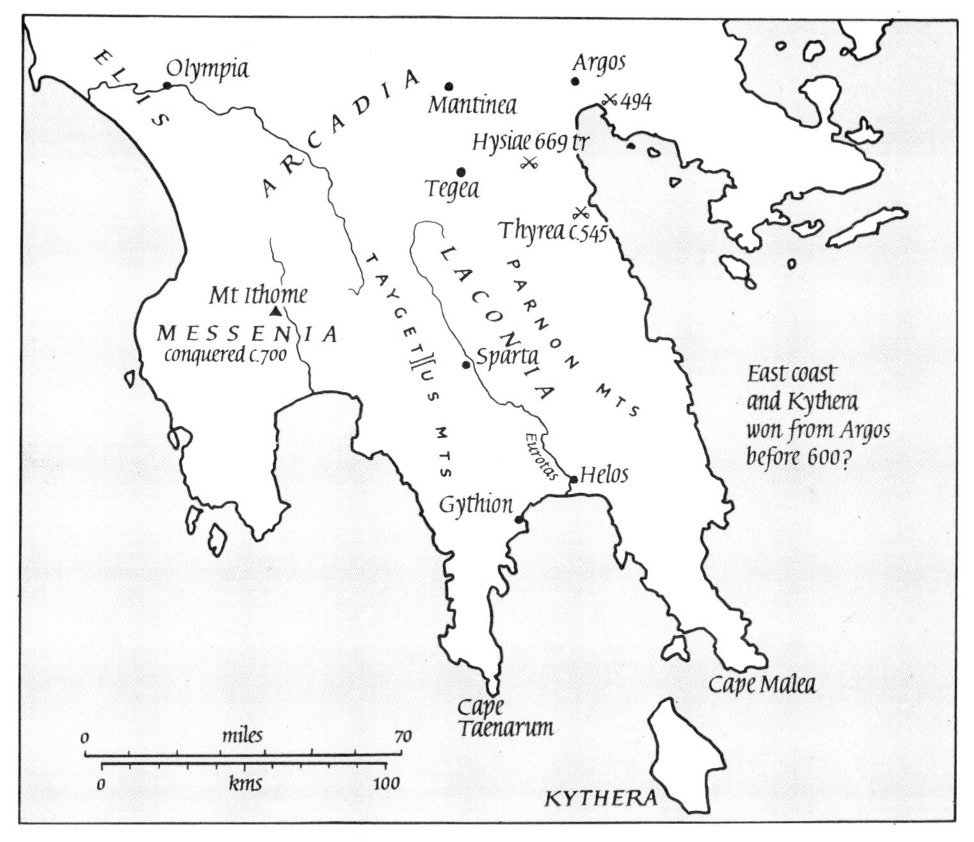

59 The mountain-girdled plain; the citadel of unwalled Sparta's military power

Celtic king, is thought to be sixth-century Spartan work. Nor did either Sparta or Crete make any contribution to Greek thought or literature. In both, society had been 'frozen' in an archaic form, in the interests of military efficiency and the maintenance of privilege.

Peculiar to Sparta was the severe military and athletic training of the boys, who were taken from their mothers at the age of seven and brought up in 'packs', each under a selected young man for whom the boys 'fagged', the whole being under the direction of a respected older citizen. They plucked their own bedding of reeds from the River Eurotas; they had no extra clothes for winter,

Ill. 62

60 The bronze Vix Crater or 'mixer' (for mixing their strong wine with water, as Greeks always did) stands $5\frac{1}{2}$ feet high, and apart from its artistic merit the industrial competence that could produce it, and the ability to move it to a Celtic stronghold in Burgundy, overlooking the Upper Seine, is impressive

61, 62 *Above*, a detail from the crater (*opposite*). The figures, six inches high, were cast separately and attached in marked positions. The infantry will have had detachable spears, which have perished. The art is considered by experts to be in the Spartan tradition and of about 520; though it has been suggested that the Spartan colony of Taranto, which had had no 'Lycurgan' reform, is a possible place of origin. *Below*, from the same school as the Arkesilas Cup (*Ill. 32*), but in a very different spirit, this homecoming of Spartan warriors with their dead breathes the atmosphere of the austere, military community

and food was of the plainest, a kind of wheat porridge; they were encouraged to supplement it by stealing from the farms, and punished if caught, being held to deserve it for bad scouting. Any weakly babies, who looked unlikely to survive this treatment, were not brought up at all; they were put out to die on Mount Taygetus. Men continued to live a 'Spartan' life, in their messes; failure to be elected to a mess was social and political death. They passed their time in military training, hunting and supervising the helots on their farms, visiting their wives in the log-cabins that were their homes only by stealth. Sparta never coined money, keeping for currency the prehistoric system of iron currency-bars, too cumbersome for anyone to accumulate. Trade and manufacture were left to the 'dwellers-around', the free but non-Spartiate men of other villages and townships in the plain and on the coasts of Laconia. Girls also underwent an athletic training, intended to fit them to be the mothers of warriors; and for both them and the men and boys, life

63 Iron spits, the 'currency' that Sparta retained. The Greek for a spit was *obelos*, and six of them made a 'handful' (*drachma*); and both words remained in use among Greeks who adopted silver coinage

64, 65 Pre-'reformation' Sparta had even had artists who signed their work (probably Laconian 'dwellers-around' rather than Spartiate full citizens). This head, *left*, decoration for a handle of a bronze *hydria* (water-pot) is signed by one Telestas. *Right*, the archaic Spartan girl athlete, holding up the front of her short 'gym-frock' the better to run, is one of a few that commemorate this practice. The same word, *gymnos*, was used to mean either 'naked' or 'lightly clad', in tunic only, and that Spartan girls exercised in public stark naked is probably a misunderstanding. But it is true that Athenians, who kept their young ladies sheltered, thought Spartan practices immodest

was sweetened by much choral dancing and singing, especially at religious festivals.

The government of this community was a limited monarchy: limited, firstly, by the curious fact that Sparta from the first had two royal families, which were usually in rivalry; secondly, by a council of twenty-eight old aristocrats, elected when over sixty, for life (some of them therefore always senile); and thirdly, and more effectively, by the five Ephors (Overseers), elected annually by and from among the whole body of some ten thousand male Spartiates (a number which later declined). Originally these represented the Spartan people's safeguard against despotism; but as time passed, they acquired more and more power, until they were in a position to call kings to account for misconduct and even, if supported by the Assembly, to exile or depose them. The kings' chief sphere of activity was in the command of the army (only one at a time – after a serious quarrel between two kings in the field, in 507), and in foreign affairs, in which they often showed, it must be said, wider views and more generosity than were characteristic of the Spartan Assembly and Ephors.

The Lycurgan system gave Sparta a professional army (the only one in Greece), which could be reinforced with useful though non-professional forces of the 'dwellers-around'. With it, though still, fortunately for herself, unable to conquer Arcadia and saddle herself with still more helots, Sparta humbled her old rival, Argos, and organized the rest of the Peloponnese – including Arcadia, Elis in the west, Corinth, Megara, Sicyon and the smaller neighbours of Argos – into a League of Allies, pledged to follow Sparta in foreign policy. The League was an element of stability in Greece, and was to do good service against the danger from the east; but it was a stability of conservatism and reaction. The whole Peloponnese contributed, except in sculpture, relatively little to the constructive Classical Greek achievement. This achievement was, in many of its greatest triumphs, the work of Athens.

CHAPTER FOUR

Athens: The Struggle for Democracy

Athens' history before 600 is almost a blank; but this does not mean that she was a negligible quantity. Her art – her Geometric pottery and, later, her first monumental sculpture – was already the best in all Greece. The fact was simply that she did not colonize and had no revolution. With a thousand square miles of territory, much more of a 'country' than that of most Greek states, her population had not yet reached saturation-point. Down to 600 she was still exporting grain.

Ills 66–68

But that critical point was now being reached, and with the coming of coined money and the facilitation thereby of usury and debt, there was, here too, a formidable social crisis. More and more of the poorer farmers fell into debt to the rich nobles; and unpaid debt meant that, in the last resort, not only the debtor's land but his body and those of his family belonged to the creditor. His usual fate, rather than to be kept as a resentful servant, was to be sold overseas, *e.g.* to the slave-economy of Aegina, a fate from which even Sparta's helots were exempt. There was bitter discontent, and while the rich, with the best arms, could probably have crushed any revolt, they could also see that the elimination of the middling peasantry, or their depression into the ranks of those who could not afford armour, weakened the whole state.

Ills 10, 54

66 The great funerary vases, some five feet high, with every inch of space meticulously decorated, which stood over graves outside the later Dipylon Gate, are a reminder that Athenian nobles even in the eighth century did not lack surplus wealth to spend on artistic work. The mourning scene, as always in the Dipylon tradition, carefully shows the corpse as well as the pall that would in reality have covered it

67, 68 The magnificent *kouros* ('youth'), *left*, from Cape Sunium, ten feet high, was set up before 600 BC. So confident was Athenian art, even then. Probably all these *kouroi* represent (not portray) young men of noble families dead before their time, often in war. Indeed, the later figure, *right* (*c*. 540; from Anávysos, near the south coast of Attica), had an inscription on its base: 'Stay! Spare a thought for Croesus, slain before his time, in the front rank, by furious War.' The non-Greek name Croesus suggests a family desirous to honour Croesus the Lydian (p. 80); very likely that Alcmeonid family, to which Cleisthenes the reformer (p. 77) belonged, and whose enrichment by Croesus is described in an amusing story by Herodotus

In these circumstances the Athenian nobles showed some wisdom. They agreed to the election of Solon with dictatorial powers as head of state in the year 594 or 592 BC. He was a noble of royal descent but modest wealth, who had seen the world abroad as a merchant and had written poems vigorously attacking the greed of the rich. All Athens swore to obey whatever measures he should introduce. Solon then proceeded to cancel all debts outstanding; to lay down that no man should ever again be enslaved for debt; and to buy back with public funds all those enslaved abroad who could be traced. He also forbade the export of corn, thus keeping at home the

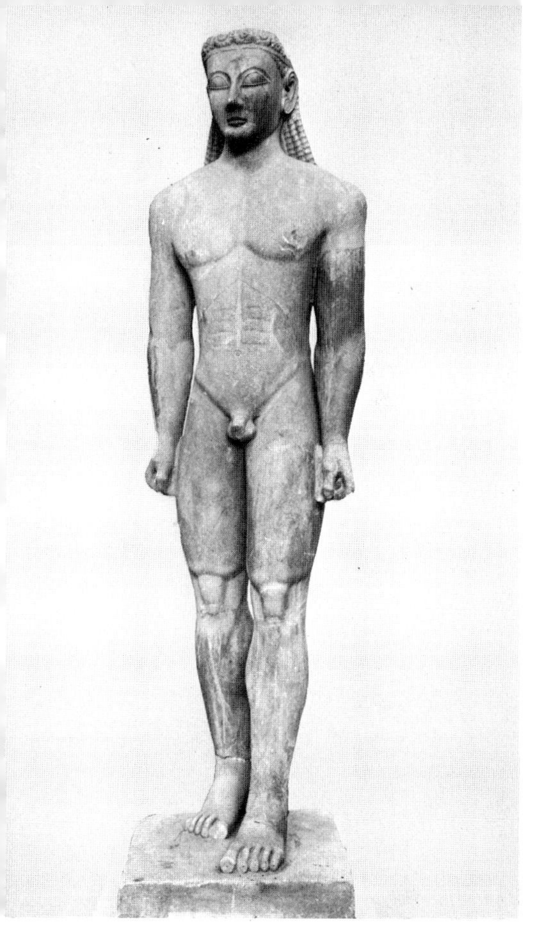

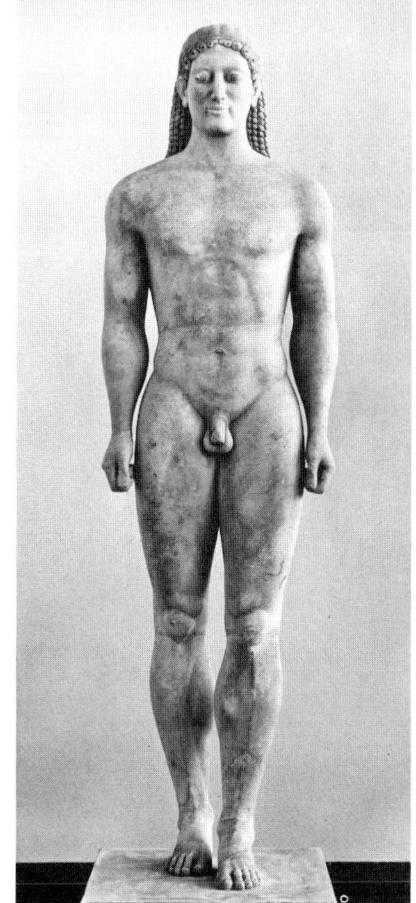

grain that might otherwise have commanded a higher price in Chalcis or Aegina, and lowering the home price. This stimulated the cultivation of the vine and the olive which can grow on stony hill-slopes; and olive-oil became a mainstay of Athenian export trade.

Next, Solon drastically reformed the constitution. He laid down that all free men, even the landless, should be admitted to the Assembly (not, as in some states, only those who could afford armour), and that the nine annual Archons (chief Archon or Regent, 'King' for religious affairs, War-chief and six junior judicial Archons), though they still had to belong to the equestrian class, should be elected by that Assembly; further, that after their year of office they should be accountable to the Assembly, and that only if the account was accepted should they pass for life into the august Council of ex-Archons, which meeting on (or perhaps rather, under) the Rock of Ares, the war-god, was called the Council of Areopagus. Further, the Assembly could also function as a People's Court, to hear complaints against or on behalf of individuals; and Solon provided that 'anyone who wished' (not only a kinsman) might take up the case of anyone wronged; a safeguard of the rights of the poor and inarticulate, and especially of the orphan and widow.

If, however, all the preliminary discussion of public affairs and the decision as to what business should be laid before the Assembly, and how, and when, continued to be the business of the 'best people', that is to say of the Areopagus, it would usually be possible for the 'best people' to get their way in the Assembly, as the Senate long did at Rome. Solon saw this, and with great acumen provided against it. He introduced a new, second or people's council, later called The Council, for the express purpose of preparing the Assembly's business. It consisted of four hundred (later five hundred) citizens, selected annually *by lot* from among all who volunteered to serve and who passed a summary scrutiny to ensure that they were citizens in good standing. The Areopagus was left with the function of 'protecting the laws'; it was the supreme court for homicide (preventing blood feuds) and could proceed against revolutionaries; but it lost the power of controlling the Assembly by acting as its steering committee. Also, the laws were written up in public; they were no longer to be known only to aristocratic judges.

This was not yet democracy; the Archons still had to be rich men, and in practice usually belonged to the old families; but the people gained some control over their

69 The characteristic features of a warship – sharp ram, high prow and stern-posts, oars swinging together, shields above – are emphasized on this accomplished chalcedony gem

government. The name of Solon was rightly revered by later democrats.

Solon's laws did not give Athens peace. They were followed by faction struggles between 'Coast' and 'Plain', the commercial section against inland aristocrats, and between great men contending for the Archonship or, in one case, for re-election to it. In the end, Athens had a 'tyrant' after all: Pisistratus, a popular nobleman and general, who organized a third party among the still poor upland peasants. After many adventures he seized power for the third time about 546 BC, and held it until his death in 528. He ruled from a 'back seat', controlling elections, while the Assembly continued to function, under the Laws of Solon. He raised a direct tax of ten per cent on farm produce, made loans to peasants on easy terms for the improvement of their equipment, and had the satisfaction of seeing production soar. Athens already had a navy, though not at this time a very large one; and Pisistratus secured outposts for Athens on both sides of the Dardanelles, on the way to the great source of grain supplies on the Black Sea.

Ills 69, 70

His son Hippias remained in power until 510; but as usual, with the revolution's most pressing work done, the new despot's popularity waned. His brother was assassinated in a private quarrel, and Hippias was finally turned out by Sparta, after another Athenian nobleman turned businessman, Cleisthenes (he took the contract for rebuilding the temple at Delphi after a fire), had used his influence at Delphi to get the Oracle to put pressure on Sparta.

Cleisthenes, whose father had married the daughter of Cleisthenes of Sicyon, finding himself faced by a clubful of more conservative nobles, then 'took the people into his club' (it was probably his disgusted opponents who said it first), carrying through the Assembly a Bill which made all free men of Athens, about whose citizenship

70 Of all our numerous representations of Greek ships (always excepting the three-banked trireme, whose oars were hard to show) this sixth-century black-figure cup best emphasizes the contrast between merchantman and warship, or 'round ship' and 'long ship' as the ancients put it; the latter sleek and rakish, the former roomy for freight and depending on sail alone

there was any doubt, citizens by Act of Parliament. As there had been much immigration from Ionia, since the conquest by Persia (see below), and since no one had bothered greatly about voting-rolls under the tyrants, there were by now many among the townsfolk of Athens, the legal or marital status of whose grandparents may have been uncertain. Solon had provided that an immigrant, who came with his family, and practised a useful trade, could become a citizen; but the conservatives would have liked to eliminate as many as possible and keep the Assembly in the hands of solid Athenian countrymen who would vote with the squire. To make

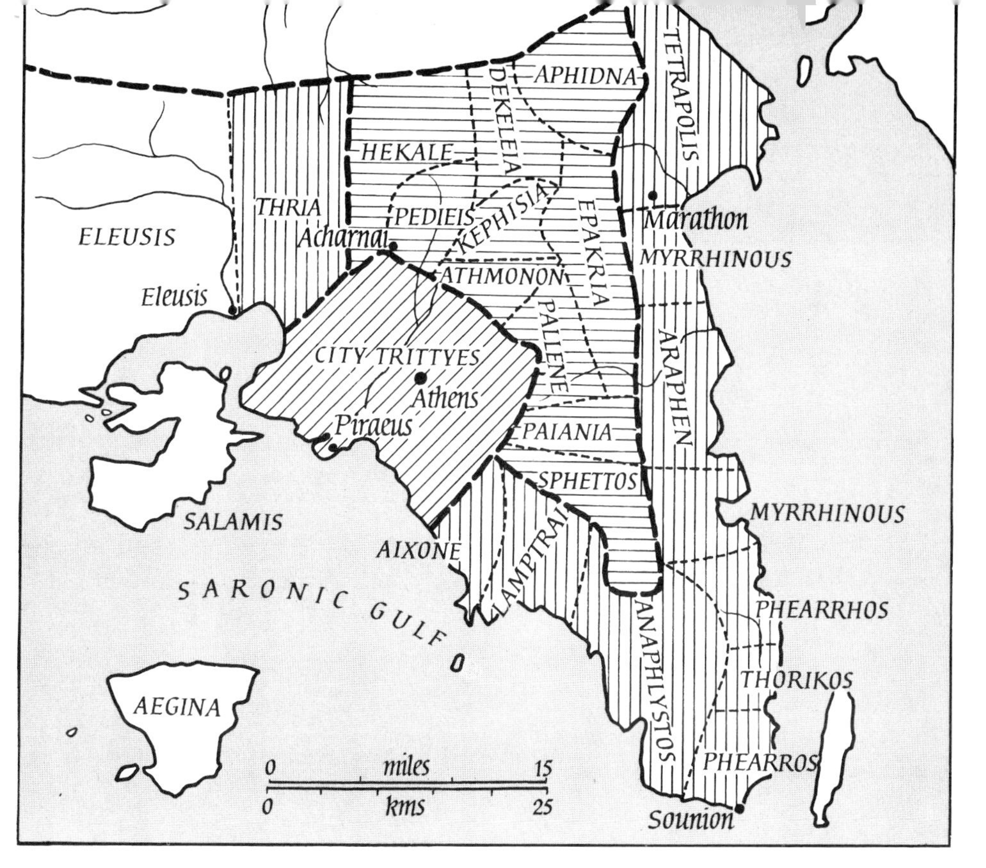

71 Cleisthenes' redrawing of the political map has something in common with that carried out by the French Revolution, officially abolishing the old Provinces and centralizing the country. Even Cleisthenes' regions are not the same as the old ones; his Inland 'Third' includes both Plain and Upland, and both the old Plain and Coast factions were strongly represented in his City area

return impossible, Cleisthenes abolished the Ionic 'tribes' of Athens and substituted ten new ones, named after ancient Attic kings and heroes; and to consolidate the country and get rid of the local factions of Plain, Coast and Upland, he made his tribes highly artificial, each containing a group of wards or villages, called a Third, (*a*) from the city and environs, (*b*) from the coast, and (*c*) from inland. He did not alter most of the constitutional arrangements of Solon; but he made the voting body much larger, and much more radical. It was the Athens of Cleisthenes that fought the great Persian War to keep the East at bay.

Ill. 71

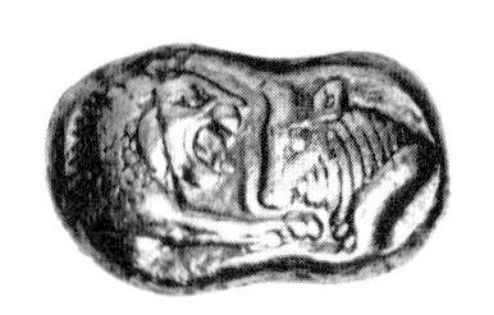

72 Gold coins of Croesus still remained roughly shaped stamped lumps gold, at a time when Greeks had already adopted the circular shape. Here, the observe type shows a lion and a bull facing each other, the reverse is is a simple punch-mark

The Persian Threat: Marathon

Assyria, exhausted by her own conquests, had perished; Nineveh fell to the Medes, who had learned the art of war from Assyria herself, in 612 BC; and the empire was divided between the Medes and the Chaldaeans, a people of the Arabian desert-edge who had gained power in Babylon (Nebuchadrezzar, 605–562). But in 550 Cyrus, King of the Persians, a vassal people akin to the Medes, overthrew his overlord and made his own nation dominant. The Greeks saw little difference between them, and often called Persians Medes.

Cyrus was a man of genius. Braving a late autumn campaign in Anatolia, he conquered Croesus of Lydia in 547, and his generals soon subdued Ionia; aided by disaffection within (the 'second Isaiah' hails him as the Lord's Anointed), he took Babylon in 539; he had added the whole of Iran before he was killed fighting in central Asia in 530. His son Cambyses conquered Egypt in 525, defeating an army containing many Greek mercenaries. He died in mysterious circumstances, and the whole empire flew apart in rebellion; but by 519 the young Darius, a distant cousin of Cambyses, had suppressed all revolts and rivals. Most of his long reign was spent in a fine work of imperial organization; but in 499 came an event which cost Athens dearly. Ionia and Cyprus rebelled against the tyrants used as city governors by Persia, and were only reduced after a severe struggle lasting for six years. Miletus was sacked, and was never again a power in the world. Sparta had refused help; Athens, though bitterly divided over resistance or appeasement, had sent modest help in 498, only to withdraw it after a defeat. But Persia had been provoked; the Athenians had raided inland and sacked Sardis. A sea-borne punitive expedition crossed the Aegean in 490, winning most of the islands for Persia. It was beaten off at Marathon in one of the proudest feats of Athenian

Ills 72, 73

Ill. 78

Ill. 76

Ills 74, 75

Ills 77, 79–82

73 Herodotus says that Cyrus decided to burn Croesus alive, but then relented. This vase by Myson (*c.* 500 BC) shows Croesus preparing to immolate *himself*. The poet Bacchylides tells the same story, adding that Apollo miraculously wafted him away to the happy land of the Hyperboreans. Greeks clearly shrank from believing that one so generous and pious had really come to a bad end

74, 75 Soldiers of the Persian Wars, which Aeschylus describes as a conflict of the Spear against the Bow. The vigorous little bronze from Dodona has lost only its spear. To the right, the vivid frieze of glazed tiles shows men of the Persian Imperial Guard: the Ten Thousand 'Immortals', so called because there was never a vacancy in their ranks. These gorgeous soldiers were brave and resourceful fighters, whose capacity to move fast and to keep closed up over mountain trails in the dark was decisive at Thermopylae

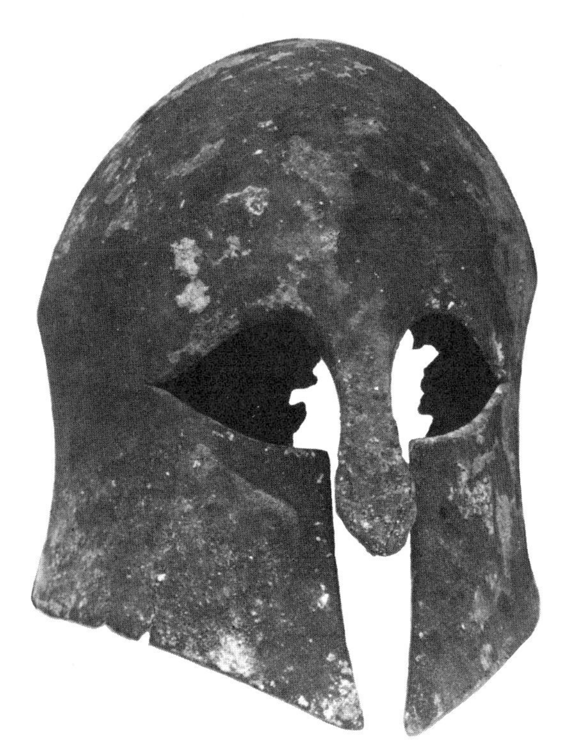

76, 77 This helmet, of the widely popular Corinthian type (*cf. Ill. 74*), is a relic of the Cypriot campaign in the Ionian revolt, which ended with a series of sieges. Excavations at Paphos revealed the siege-mound with which the Persians had filled the ditch and thrown up a ramp against the mud-brick city wall, throwing into it numerous statues and architectural blocks, evidently from tombs outside the city; and in the associated debris this Greek helmet also came to light

Opposite, the armoured trumpeter, from an Athenian black-figure plate, is a generation earlier; but the superbly spirited drawing makes it an appropriate illustration to any account of the years in which Athens defied the rulers of the east

arms, directed by Miltiades, a great soldier, once lord of the Gallipoli Peninsula under Hippias. But a greater Persian effort against Greece was bound to come.

Fortunately for Greece, there was a ten-year respite. Egypt revolted (486–485); Darius died in 486; Babylon was in revolt in 482; and meanwhile Athens found a great leader, the democrat Themistocles.

Ill. 84

Themistocles may have owed his citizenship to Cleisthenes, for, while his father came of an ancient family, his mother is said to have been foreign. He had probably already been Chief Archon in 493, and commanded the regiment of his tribe at Marathon. He then probably backed an important constitutional change, made in 487, by which the Archons, including even the War-chief, were to be appointed like the Councillors, by lot among approved candidates. It was a radical change indeed. It meant that future Archons would rarely be formidable personalities (fewer rivals for Themistocles?);

78 On the wall of the eastern doorway of the Tripylon (Triple Portal) at Persepolis, King Darius sits enthroned, with his sceptre; and the standing figure behind him may be confidently identified as the Crown Prince Xerxes

79, 80 The red-figure plate, *c.* 520–515, *below right*, with the inscription 'Miltiades [is] beautiful', might have been thus 'dedicated' to the future hero of Marathon as a young aristocrat in Athens; and indeed the subject, a horse-archer in Scythian or East Thracian dress, *might* be meant for the young Miltiades himself, whose family were lords of the Thracian Chersonese (this hypothesis is more hazardous). *Below left*, an eastern conical helmet (of a type already popular with the Assyrians) from Olympia, with the inscription: 'THE ATHENIANS DEDICATED THIS, AS SPOIL FROM THE PERSIANS'

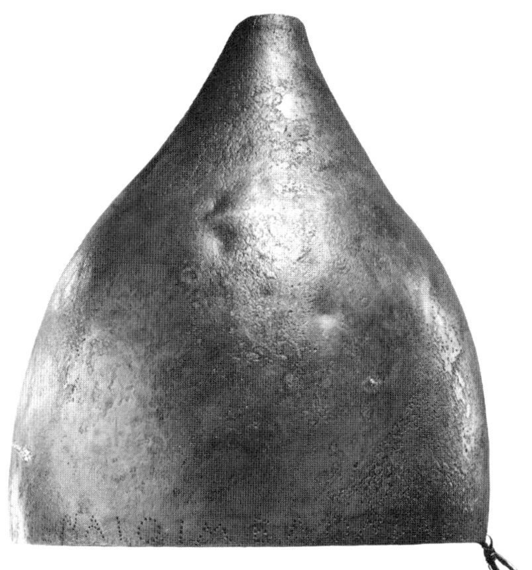

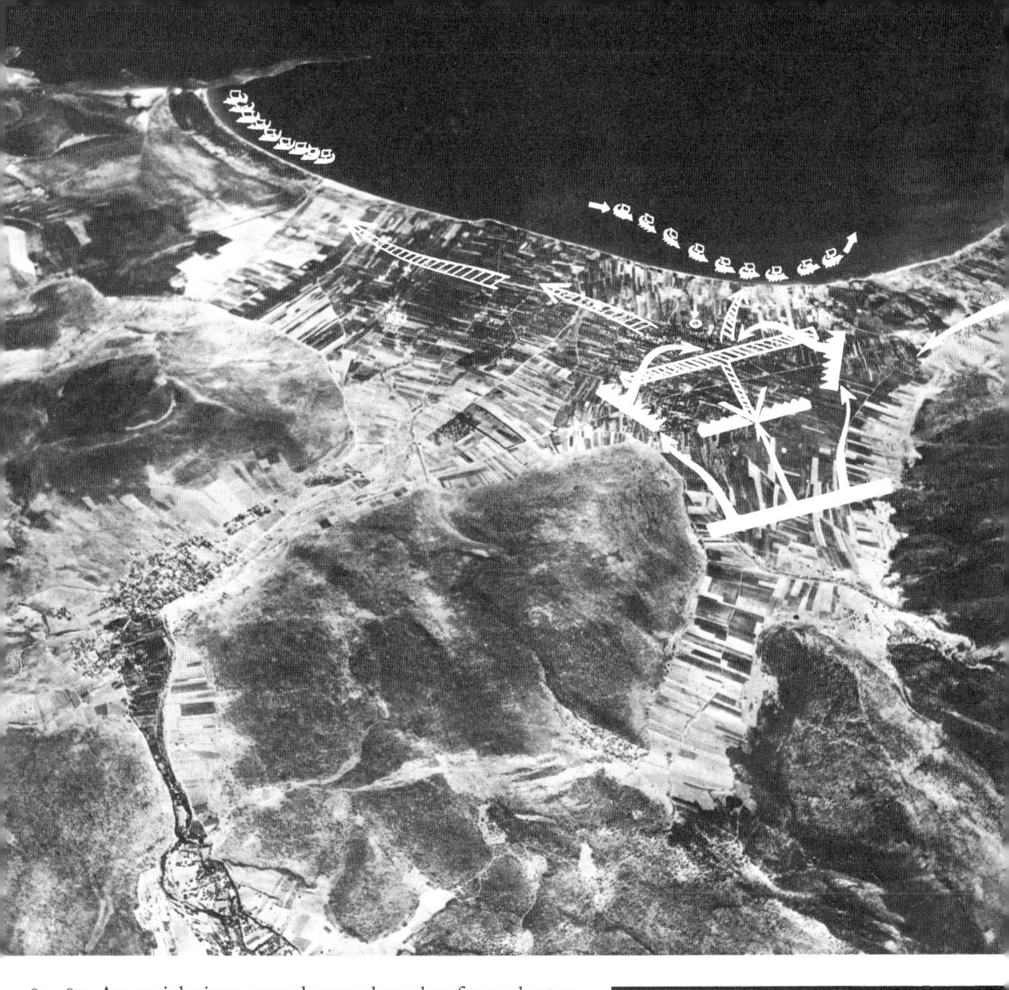

81, 82 An aerial view, even better than that from the top of Mount Pentelikos, shows the configuration of the historic Plain of Marathon. The cultivable plainland shows clearly, with the small strips and rectangles of peasant tillage (and olives, centre). COURSE OF THE BATTLE: Miltiades, not having enough men to cover the whole enemy front in depth, and knowing that if he merely pierced its centre his troops would be exposed to arrow-fire from both flanks, massed his main force on the wings, with orders to sweep away the Persian wings (consisting of half-hearted Ionian Greeks), and *converge*. This they did, to meet in rear of the native Persians, who had broken through the thin Athenian centre and were pursuing it. Cut off from the sea nearest to them, the Persians fled for their camp at the far end of the plain, but were killed in large numbers at a point where the plain was marshy, with only a narrow strip of firm going between it and the sea. *Right*, perhaps even more dramatic is the Greek helmet (its crown sadly crushed during the centuries when it lay buried) at Olympia, with the clear inscription: 'MILTIADES DEDICATED [this]'

that the conservative Areopagus would lose influence as the elder statesmen died off; and that the War-chief would henceforth be a puppet in the hands of his council, the ten Generals of the tribes, who continued to be directly elected, and could be re-elected, thus gaining experience. The Generals, *strategoi*, responsible directly to the Assembly, shortly became the General Staff of Athens.

Themistocles' finest achievement, however, was the creation of the great Athenian navy. Using the desirability of crushing an old enemy, Aegina, to convert the short-sighted, he persuaded the people to apply a windfall – the discovery of a rich vein in the state-owned silver-mines near Cape Sunium – to building up the fleet from seventy galleys to two hundred. His enemies tried to get rid of him by *ostracism*; a device of Cleisthenes, under which the people might exile for ten years, without loss of status, any man who was judged so powerful as to be a

Ill. 83

83, 84 *Ostrakismós* at Athens was so-called because the voters wrote on *ostraka*, scraps of pottery, the names of their candidates for exile. Among hundreds of *ostraka* dating between 487 and 483, far the highest 'scorer' is the ultimately victorious Themistocles himself; he, evidently, was 'at risk' every year. *Opposite*, we see, above, two sherds with his name and, as was regular, his father's; one adds his parish too ('Phrearrios'). Below them come the names of Aristides the Just (who was said to have meekly written his own name to oblige one illiterate voter who did not know him), and 'Kallixenos the son of Aristonumos', a character only known to us from these documents. (The writer has made two shots, deciding that the first, upside-down on our page, was too small.) Lastly, two sherds from later in the century preserve the names of the one-time rivals, Cimon and Pericles. *Right*, the striking bust of Themistocles himself, of Roman date, from Ostia, is defended as a possible copy of a true portrait by Dr G. M. A. Richter

danger to the Republic; but Themistocles was able to concentrate the votes of his supporters, in each 'election', against his rivals, one at a time; and one after another, they went. Last to go was the 'tory democrat', Aristides the Just, who favoured defence by land; and by 480 the ships were ready, though their crews could not match the skill of the Phoenicians, who fought for Persia, on the open sea.

Victory in the Narrow Straits

In 480 King Xerxes personally led a great and carefully organized expedition round the north Aegean. Pontoon bridges had been stretched across the Dardanelles and a canal cut through the sandy neck behind Mount Athos, where an earlier Persian fleet had come to grief in a gale. In the same summer the Carthaginians invaded Sicily, but were routed at Himera by Gelon, Tyrant of Syracuse. In Greece, Athens generously and wisely conceded the

Ill. 85

85 One of the Gelon's magnificent Syracusan ten-drachma coins, with the head of the fountain-nymph Arethusa, surrounded by dolphins (the Spring on the Island), and chariot on the reverse. Being of silver, they are *not* directly identifiable with the Demareteion pieces which Gelon's wife Demarete is said to have had struck from the gold crown that the Carthaginians sent her as thank-offering for her 'good offices' after their defeat; but, it is at least a pleasant fancy, she may have sat as model for Arethusa

chief command to Sparta, not only by land (naturally) but by sea, seeing that Sparta's allies, especially Aegina, would not consent to put their fleets under an Athenian; but Themistocles was the moving spirit in Greek strategic councils. The allied fleets took post off a temple of Artemis at the north end of Euboea, where the enemy could only come at them along the mountainous coast of Thessaly, dangerous to a large fleet for lack of anchorages; and the Phoenician and other Levantine navies did indeed sustain serious losses there in another north Aegean gale; losses perhaps decisive of the result of the war. Nevertheless, they pressed on, to reach shelter in the straits opposite the Greek base; and after three days fighting (the very important but little publicized Battle of Artemisium), in which they inflicted further loss, the Greeks were fought to a standstill and had to withdraw.

Ill. 86
Ill. 87
Ill. 88

Meanwhile Leonidas, King of Sparta, with about seven thousand armoured men besides light-armed, had covered the landward flank, holding the coast road by the hot springs of Thermopylae, between cliffs and the sea;

86 This attractive though broken statue of a warrior in 'Corinthian' helmet (itself much chipped) was found at Sparta, 'opposite the theatre', where the traveller Pausanias mentions monuments to Pausanias the general at Plataea and to Leonidas. The apparently defensive attitude makes it reasonable to identify this as the hero of Thermopylae

87 This dour little bronze of a warrior is certainly of the early fifth century, and may well be of Spartan workmanship. The carefully dressed locks of hair falling from under his helmet remind us of Herodotus' story of the Spartans combing their hair under the puzzled gaze of a Persian scout, 'that they might die with their heads tidy'. Cloaked against the night air, it is easy to imagine such a grim figure on sentry duty in the moonlight before the battle in the Pass

88 The gorge of the Asopos (one of several Greek torrents so-called) emerges, a little west of the hot springs that gave Thermopylae its name, from cliffs that give a good idea of the mountain obstacle confronting invaders. Flooded after rain, in dry weather the gorge is passable, and was probably used, as well as the coastal main road, by the Persians after the battle. But it was guarded by a walled stronghold of the local Greeks on top of the cliffs, and the Persians did not attempt it until they had mastered the mountains by an easier ascent further west. The heavy fighting was on the coast road, where the sea then (but not now) almost lapped the foot of the mountains

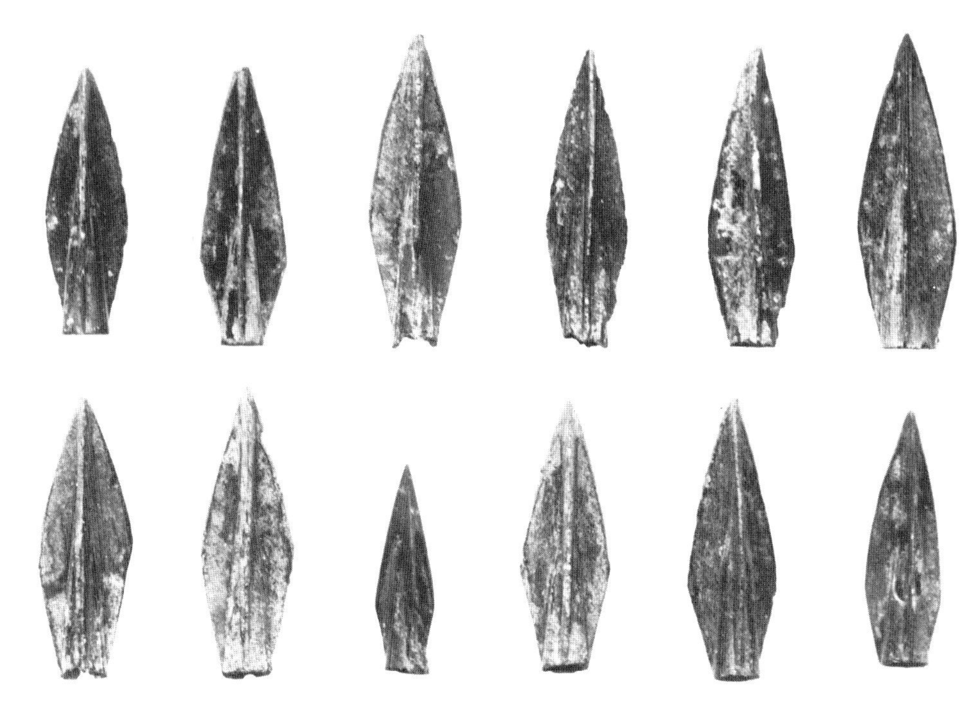

89 The Mound, east of the narrows on the coast road, where the rearguard, Spartans, Boeotians and (barely mentioned by Herodotus) helot soldiers, made their last stand, was identified by the discovery there of hundreds of bronze arrowheads, of which a few are here illustrated. Hollow-socketed and three-edged, they are of a traditional Near Eastern type, found in many places in Asia; among others, by D. G. Hogarth and T. E. Lawrence among debris of Nebuchadrezzar's battle of Carchemish

but he was left too long unreinforced, and perhaps also outgeneralled. The Persians hammered at his position regardless of losses, with the result that he kept nearly all his force on the coast road; then, experienced mountain fighters as they were, they sent their Guard division by night over hill-paths inland, with a local guide. The Greek local troops on the mountain pulled in to a peak; and the Persians ignored them and went past. Leonidas, warned by runners, sent away most of his force; he gained them time to get clear by staying himself with a sacrificed rear-guard, eleven hundred Boeotians and his personal guard, the famous three hundred Spartans.

Ill. 89

Defeated on land and sea, the Peloponnesians had no further idea but to 'dig in' on the Isthmus of Corinth. The Athenian government withdrew to Salamis; but

90 At Troizen (opposite the modern island seaside resort of Poros), to which many Athenians evacuated their families in the critical summer of 480, there came to light this modest slab, scarred by ploughshares while lying buried. In 1957 M. H. Jameson identified at its top the much-defaced name of Themistocles, and realized that it bears what purports to be the text of his mobilization decree, moved in the Athenian Assembly in spring of 480; a text already known in part through quotation by a popular lecturer of the Roman Empire. The stone was set up as part of a patriotic memorial in the late fourth or third century, when Athens and Troizen were once more allied, against Macedonia; but how old is the text? It is hardly a copy of a contemporary inscription; those of the Persian War period are all short, and nearly all metrical. Nor is it likely that Athens at that time preserved its papers; but there is evidence that in the fourth century alleged documents of the Great War were being 'restored' and quoted for patriotic purposes. As what Athens a century later thought Themistocles said or should have said, the inscription is of interest

Themistocles persuaded the allied fleet to put in there too, first to help with the evacuation and then to defend the island, now an important military objective. The Persian fleet, weakened by its losses in storm and battle, could no longer afford to divide its forces; and Themistocles by a deceitful message to Xerxes, pretending to turn traitor and emphasizing the (real) divisions among the allies, induced him to order it into the Salamis strait in an all-out attack. There the Athenians enveloped the head of its column, the Phoenicians, while the Peloponnesians attacked the following divisions in flank: the Greeks are said to have destroyed or taken two hundred ships, for the loss of forty; and Xerxes, probably unable to supply his large army without command of the sea, withdrew with most of it to Asia. He left a picked army of occupation

Ill. 90

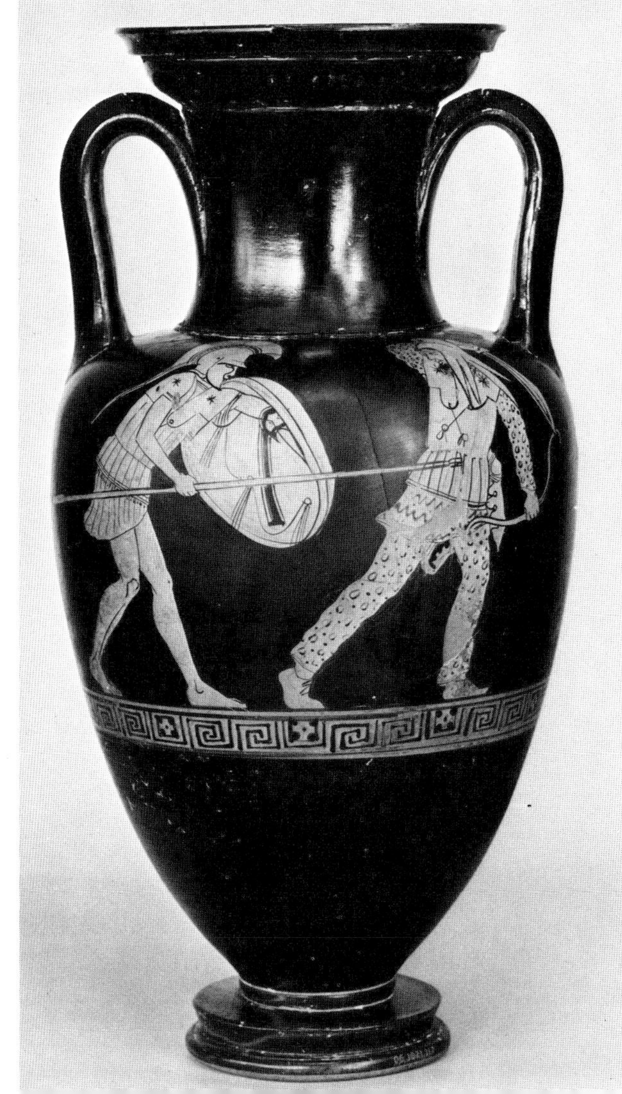

91 One of the rare ten-drachma pieces of Athens, and probably a victory issue of 478–477. Athena (as since Marathon) wears the bay leaves of victory and her owl, rather comically, spreads its wings in triumph

92 The spear defeats the bow; a Greek spears a Persian, an incident repeated thousands of times on the field of Plataea, when the Spartans, after standing stoically under arrow-fire until the Persians were close-massed in front of them, charged into the mass

93 The Serpent Column. The Greek War Memorial was a bronze column of three twining serpents, their heads supporting a golden tripod (sacrificial cauldron). It was set up before the Temple at Delphi, but has now stood for some sixteen hundred years in the Hippodrome of Constantinople. For inscription, it bore originally the name of Pausanias the Spartan Regent and general as dedicator; but the Spartans, indignant at this egoism, had it erased, and substituted the names of thirty-one cities, with the truly 'laconic' comment: 'These fought the war'

in northern Greece under Mardonius, his chief marshal; but the Greeks (not until the Athenians had threatened to make peace if they were left unsupported) destroyed it at Plataea in Boeotia in 479. Meanwhile, a Greek fleet destroyed the Persian remnants at Cape Mycale in Ionia.

Ills 91–93

The Athenian Empire

The Greek cities of Asia were now liberated again, with support almost entirely from Athens. Athens hastily rebuilt her walls, against the will of Sparta, which would have liked to keep her dependent. Sparta, hampered by internal troubles and soon by wars at home, with Argos and most of Arcadia, withdrew from assisting in the work; and it was the Athenian, Aristides the Just, who drew up the charter of a new League, with its headquarters at Delos. Athens and the liberated cities swore alliance 'for ever', for their mutual protection and to wage war on Persia. It was the opinion of many, and not least of Athens' rising soldier, Cimon the son of Miltiades, that such a war could be made to pay.

Ill. 94

This Delian League became an Athenian Empire. From the first, Athens was accepted as 'managing director', providing the high command, choosing objectives and controlling the Treasury. It was reasonable from the first that the smaller cities (there were over two hundred in all), whose share of a League fleet of a hundred or two hundred galleys was a fraction of a ship, should commute for a money payment, while their young men served, if they chose, in Athenian ships for pay. Soon only a few preserved independent forces. Athens protected them; but on what terms became evident when some of the larger (Naxos *c.* 467, Thasos 465), feeling that liberation was now secure, tried to secede. Athens, with legal right (for the alliance was 'for ever'), coerced them. The moral rights of this have been a subject of debate ever since.

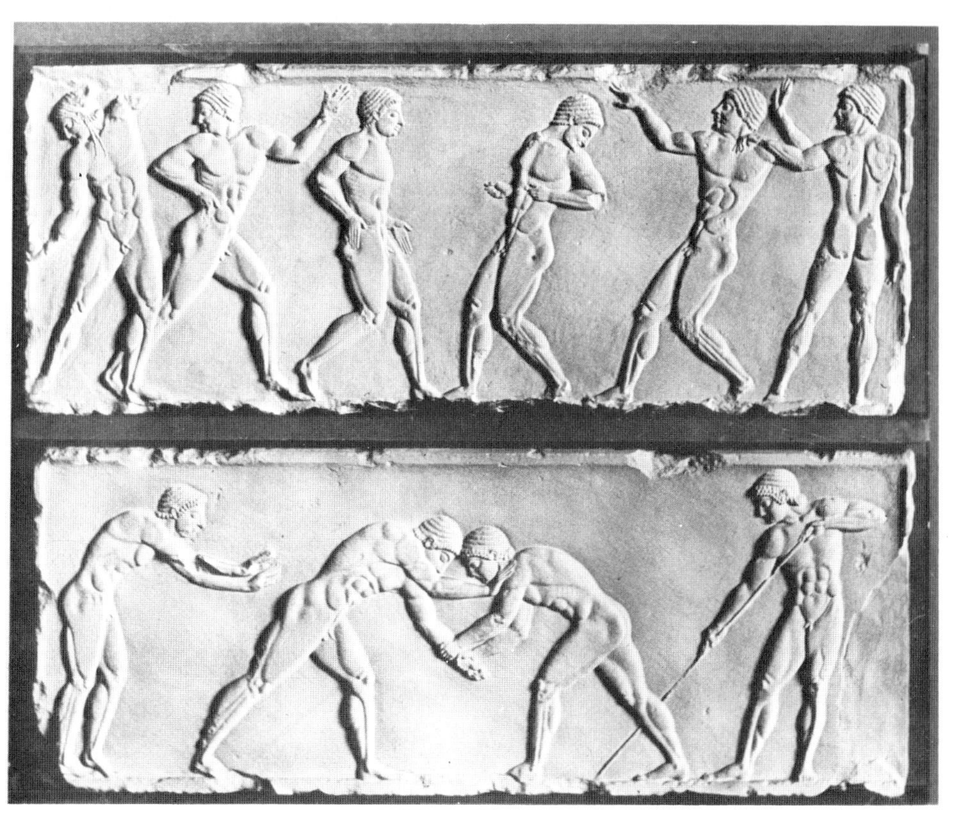

94 A team ball-game, a sport hardly mentioned in Classical literature, is shown above on a relief from one of the statue bases, which the Athenians built into their walls when hastily restoring them in 479–478. *Below*, a wrestler attempts the 'flying mare' throw, which his opponent parries

Soon Athens extended her power west of the Aegean; she protected Megara against Corinth, defeated Corinth's and Aegina's united navies, besieged Aegina and forced her to join the League. For ten years, 457–447 BC, she even controlled Boeotia. But her power wilted after her most ambitious eastern enterprise, supporting a new rebellion in Egypt, ended with an army and fleet being trapped in the Nile and lost (454). Athens never again willingly fought Persians and Peloponnesians simultaneously, as she had done before; and when Boeotia rebelled in 447, and Megara, now with support from Corinth, in 446, she was powerless to win them back.

Ill. 95

Meanwhile, after Cimon had died of sickness in a last and unsuccessful attempt to liberate Cyprus, Athens had

95, 96 *Left*, the 'Mourning Athena': an exquisite little marble relief on the Acropolis, mid-fifth century, shows the goddess reading an inscription; no doubt a list of the fallen in a campaign. (We have several such lists.) *Right*, a later copy of the best-known portrait of Pericles, probably a good if idealized likeness. The pupils of the eyes would be rendered in paint

made peace with Persia (449). This led to a major crisis in the Empire, since the cities expected that their contributions, levied for the conduct of war, would now be suspended. But Athens was faced with the problem of converting her economy, long a war economy financed out of those contributions, to a peace footing. The solution adopted was that of a great programme of temple-building and other public works; and for this she needed the contributions and continued to levy them, arguing that, as long as she kept Persia at arm's length and policed the Aegean, she was doing what she was paid for. This was the political and economic background of the great buildings on the Athenian Acropolis.

Ill. 97

The author of this argument of very dubious morality, as some Athenians said at the time, was Pericles, son of Xanthippus (Athens' admiral at Mycale), by a niece of Cleisthenes, and for many years Athens' leading statesman and general. He had come to the fore first in 461 as the lieutenant of Ephialtes, a fierce and austere democrat, who completed the democratization of the city, stripping the Areopagus of its power, as 'guardian of the laws' – a supreme court – to interfere with legislation: a logical sequel to the reform of 487.

Ill. 96

Pericles was the most brilliant of numerous Athenian aristocrats who served the democracy, filling many of the ten posts of general year by year, and prominent in the Assembly, though often harried there by demagogues (the word is Athenian), popular leaders, mostly of the business class, who took it upon themselves to see that the gentry did not have things all their own way. Pericles was a convinced liberal and democrat, and gained the confidence of the Assembly as no later Athenian was ever to do. But he was also a convinced imperialist. When Euboea revolted in 446 (just before Megara), he personally led the army which crushed it, after buying off a Peloponnesian invasion with a promise to negotiate, backed by a secret bribe to the Spartan king and his chief of staff; an episode which cost the young Spartan king his throne. He then made peace (445), ceding Megara and other points on the mainland, but keeping Euboea, Aegina and the rest of Athens' naval empire.

The Classical Flowering

The exciting developments of seventh- and sixth-century Greek culture had sprung, as we saw, from an age of expansion and revolution in the world of the city-states, and radiated from the Central Aegean area, from the Isthmus region to the west coast of Asia Minor. That of the fifth century is centred solely in imperial Athens.

The period of the Persian domination of eastern Greece and threat to the west had not been sterile. It was the age of Pythagoras, Xenophanes and Heracleitus (p. 65). Lyric poetry culminated in the earlier work of Pindar the Theban, with his great odes for athletes, and of Simonides of Ceos, who came to the court of Hippias and lived on to write several and be credited later with more of the classic epitaphs on the fallen of the Persian Wars. At Athens, under Hippias and the early democracy, archaic art culminated in the delicate *korai* (maidens) of the Acropolis, girl acolytes of Athena. They were found where they were buried, after being thrown down in the Persian sack. Vase painters invented the new red-figure technique, giving more scope for the rendering of internal detail, drawn in on the 'reserved' figures. It was the age of the little-known beginnings of the dramatic or costumed-oratorio religious performances known as Tragedy ('Song at the Goat-sacrifice'?) and given at festivals of the vegetation-god Dionysus.

Ill. 99

Ill. 91

Aeschylus, who fought in the Persian Wars and commemorated that, not his poetry, in his own epitaph, is the master with whom tragedy comes into our view, first with *The Persians* (472 BC), commemorating the triumph of Salamis. He is contemporary with the emergence of the classic style in sculpture, grave where the archaic was gay. Life is serious. Tragedy, the culmination of Greek poetry, with all the experience of Homer and the choral lyric behind it, is characteristic also of the splendours and tensions of the Athenian Empire.

One generation saw the great work of Aeschylus and Early Classical art carried on to full maturity in the tragedies of Sophocles (a general along with Pericles in 440), the sculptures of Pheidias, who worked on the Parthenon, and the architecture of Ictinus and Callicrates, who built that temple, and Mnesicles the architect of the entrance-portals of the Acropolis, the Propylaea. Athens

Ills 100, 101

Ill. 97

was not the only home of Classical culture. Sicily, victorious against Carthage, was also building splendid temples – those of Acragas (Agrigento) still stand – and Pindar, Simonides and Aeschylus (who died in Sicily) all visited and wrote for the soldier-tyrants of Acragas and Syracuse. Ionian philosophy and science were carried on by Leucippus of Miletus, proposer of an atomic theory of matter, further developed by Democritus (*c.* 470–380) at Abdera on the coast of Thrace. Democritus' contemporary Hippocrates, the father of European medicine, worked on his native Cos, and an older Hippocrates, a great mathematician, at Chios. But increasingly, leading intellectuals were drawn to visit Athens; among them, if we may believe Plato, Parmenides from Elea, an Ionian colony in Italy, father of an austere and mystical monism inspired by hints from Xenophanes, with his disciple Zeno, who had developed logical disputation to show that a 'common-sense' view of things produced just as many difficulties; and certainly Herodotus from Halicarnassus, whose great history of the Persian Wars begins with a long introduction, by far our best and most readable source for Greek and Near Eastern history in the previous two centuries. Pheidias, meanwhile, was invited to make the great gold and ivory Zeus at Olympia.

Ill. 98

Ill. 102

Now too there flocked to Athens from all sides *sophists*, *i.e. teachers* of the doctrines of the philosophers, and sometimes their own too, who provided the first adult education. Since the philosophers both differed from each other and were critical of the old mythology, the result of their teaching, for the well-to-do young men who could afford their fees, tended to be a far-reaching scepticism. Old men, and young tories, like the great comic dramatist Aristophanes (born *c.* 445), deplored both the scepticism and a real or alleged decay of morals that accompanied it. The fact that the original thinkers of a hundred years had failed to arrive at agreed answers

97 'The thing which chiefly shows tha the record of the greatness of Athens i no mere legend . . . the great buildings (Plutarch). The Parthenon, here seen from the east, owes its uniquely satisfying graciousness to the famous 'refinements' scarcely a vertical or horizontal line of the building is really straight. The floor lift a few inches in the middle, the architrave (top beam) above the columns following suit. The corner columns are slightly thicker than the others, and all the columns lean very slightly inwards. The naked eye cannot see these details, but the whole, like great music, makes its effec

98 One of the historic trees of the world The huge plane tree of Cos, while it car hardly be old enough to date, as tradition would have it, from Hippocrates' time (2,400 years ago!), may nevertheless repre sent the grove and the approximate place where the father of western medicine taught and meditated

99 The *Korai* (maidens) of the Acropolis form the principal collection among the sculptures which make the Acropolis Museum one of the most attractive in the world. Recovered by Greek archaeologists in 1885–90, from the pit between the classical fortification wall and the natural rock, where they had been put away after the Persian sack, they were among the first sculptures to make the modern world aware of the charm of Late Archaic or pre-Classical art. They were also among the first to reveal the fact, shocking to the sub-Renaissance Europe of the nineteenth century, that Greek statuary was regularly painted. This example is probably the work of a Chian; certainly it is by an Ionian artist.

These smiling ladies in their gay clothes take us back to that 'young, light-hearted' Greece that vanished in the tensions of the Persian Wars and the Athenian Empire; the Greece revealed to us in literature by the lyric poets and by Herodotus, though he himself lived in the fifth century. What or whom the statues represent is uncertain; but very likely they are girl acolytes, of leading Athenian families, whose parents may have dedicated their statues when they left the service of the goddess on marriage

100 Pheidias is said to have conceived the idea of inserting portraits of Pericles and himself among the battling Greeks on the shield of his Athena Parthenos. The practice might seem a pleasant and harmless one, and in Christian art becomes firmly established; but at Athens, probably from jealousy, Pheidias was prosecuted for 'impiety' or sacrilege, for thus mixing up the sacred and the secular, and had to leave Athens.

The Strangford Shield – a fragment of a marble copy of Pheidias' masterpiece, executed as garden sculpture for some rich Roman – shows, just as Plutarch tells us, Pheidias (left) as a bald, old man hurling a stone with both hands, and Pericles (centre), 'a handsome likeness; though his arm covered part of his face'

to the deepest problems forced their successors to go on thinking, and trying to improve their methods. The results, later 'canonized' in the works of Plato (*c.* 428–348) and Aristotle (384–322), have fascinated men in all the seventy generations from their time to ours. The experience, at the time, was often agonizing.

The last third of the great fifth century at Athens is profoundly under the influence of the Sophistic movement. Already Euripides, last of the three great tragedians (*c.* 480–405), though only fifteen years younger than Sophocles, belongs to a different generation. Sophocles at fifteen had led the boys' choir in the thanksgiving for the deliverance from Persia. Euripides grew up amid the tensions and moral problems of the time when national unity fell apart and Athens ruled her empire by force.

Ill. 103

101, 102 *Above*, riders from the Parthenon frieze. The knight, right, who is still getting ready, is one of the figures from the west end which show the procession in preparation. Details, *e.g.* the mane of the horses, show certainly the work of several master-hands, and it is uncertain whether any of them was that of Pheidias. Nevertheless, the famous frieze is the best evidence that we have of Athenian sculpture of the Pheidian age. *Below*, the graffito on the bottom of an Athenian black-glazed jug declares 'PHEIDIAS' AM I'. It was found at Olympia, at a place where Pausanias the traveller tells us that Pheidias' workshop was shown. From it, then, Pheidias poured his drink while executing his last work, the colossal gold and ivory Olympian Zeus

103, 104 Euripides and Socrates. The portraits of these two great Athenians rest perhaps on less good authority than those of the statesmen (*Ills 84, 96, 114*). That of Euripides, another copy from Italy, *may* be from a near-contemporary original; that of Socrates, said to be from Alexandria, has been suspected even of being modern. Both, however, are works of considerable imaginative insight

Ill. 104

Socrates (*c.* 469–399), mystic and moralist and with a dialectic lethal to any 'phony' thinking, spent his life seeking an ethic for rational men; but, like Euripides, he could not stomach the Olympian mythology. He said so openly; and ultimately it was for 'not believing in the gods that the City believes in' and for shaking the faith of the young that, refusing to save his life by leaving Athens, he was put to death. Thucydides (before 460 to before 400), an Athenian general exiled for failure and a historian dedicated to truth and justice, wrote with relentless rationalism the history of the great war that, supervening upon the Age of the Sophists, broke the heart of imperial Athens and her power.

CHAPTER FIVE

The Breakdown of Peace

Whatever the morality of the Athenian Empire, it offered a better hope of uniting Greece politically than any other which appeared in Classical times. Before the Egyptian disaster, it seemed as though Athens might actually do it – not without coercion. After 445, for fourteen years there was 'peaceful co-existence' between Athens, everywhere encouraging (she did not everywhere impose) democratic governments among her allies, and Sparta, favouring limited-franchise governments among hers. But there was suspicion between the two blocs, and when Corinth tried to reduce her unfilial colony of Kerkyra once again and Kerkyra appealed to Athens for aid, the peace broke down. The stubborn factor, preventing a compromise solution during two years of slow drift to war, was probably the mutual fear among the leaders of the two blocs, lest their enemies should be able to cut them off from the west with its economic potentialities, and lest neutrals or lukewarm allies, seeing them weaken, might incline to the other side. Archidamus, the veteran King of Sparta, worked for peace, but the Ephors of 431 carried the Spartan Assembly against him; and on the other side Pericles himself advised the Athenians against making any concession.

The Long War with Sparta

The war that broke out in 431 BC, a struggle between a land- and a sea-power, neither of which could deal a deadly blow to the other, was a long-drawn series largely of indecisive operations. Its fame is due to the fact that the great Thucydides, probably a grandson of Miltiades, wrote the history of it, analysing with ruthless clarity the deterioration of standards of justice and political moderation under the influence of the war spirit and of fear.

The Peloponnesians could invade Attica in overwhelming force and ruin villages and farms, but could do nothing against commercial Athens, linked to the sea by impregnable 'long walls'; even less could the Athenians do anything but take useless revenge, by raiding the coasts of the Peloponnese. Pericles counted on a draw after a few campaigns, with great loss of prestige for Sparta. But in 430 Athens was struck by a frightful calamity, a plague brought by sea from Egypt; it scarcely touched the Peloponnese, unwittingly protected by the Athenian blockade of its east coast. It raged for three years, and about a quarter of the population of Athens died of it. Pericles himself died in 429, partly probably of its after-effects.

The war dragged on. Athens missed a good opportunity of ending it on the *status quo ante*, after capturing a battalion including one hundred and twenty Spartiates, valuable hostages, on an inshore island off Pylos; Pericles was gone, and Cleon, a fiery demagogue, pressed for territorial gains. Athens was defeated with the loss of a thousand armoured men in an attempt to invade Boeotia. Brasidas, an attractive Spartan, with small forces, deprived Athens of many of her tributary cities in Chalcidice; when Athens recaptured one of them, Scione, she put all the men to death and enslaved the women and children, as, later, she did to the Dorian island of Melos, which had never belonged to her League but favoured

Ills 105–107

105 A generation before the Peloponnesian War, Athens had given asylum to a body of Messenians who, failing in a rebellion against Sparta, had held out so stubbornly in the hill-fortress of Ithome that Sparta let them depart under an armistice. The Athenians settled them at Naupactus (Lepanto) which Athens had lately taken from the piratical Locrians, and they remained there, an Athenian Gibraltar in the Corinthian Gulf, for the rest of the century. Their troops distinguished themselves in the Pylos operations, and the Winged Victory of Paeonius at Olympia is their memorial for this victory. Originally, angel-winged and with flying cloak, she seems to have stood on a sphere which was painted blue, itself mounted upon a column or high base, so that she might seem to be in the act of descending from the sky

The sculptor Paeonius, curiously enough, came from Mende in Chalcidice, one of the cities which, soon after, rebelled to join Brasidas. It was, however, soon recovered, and escaped the fate of stubborn Scione

Sparta. Peace was made at last in 421, after Cleon and Brasidas had fallen in a battle in Thrace, on the same terms which Athens could have had in 425, less Brasidas' conquests.

Many Athenians nevertheless were still bellicose, and there now rose to fame a vivid and disastrous figure: Alcibiades, a young cousin of Pericles and sometime his ward, after his father had fallen in Boeotia in 447. His appearance in the pages of Plato, especially in the *Symposium* contributes to making him, of all Athenians, one of the most intimately known. When he was a brilliant boy, Socrates, who once saved his life in battle, had tried to make something of him, but in vain. Looking to war to bring him power, wealth and the adulation which he had come to crave, he worked to involve

Athens in a war between Sparta and Argos, with unhappy results; then he took up an even more 'brilliant' and dangerous project, of which some Athenians had dreamed already: that of conquering Sicily, on the pretext of 'protecting' the smaller cities against Dorian Syracuse. Thus the Peloponnese could be attacked both from east and west. When the great expedition was about to sail, he was accused by his enemies of a sacrilege, of which he was probably not guilty; but enough past cases of disrespect for religion (very shocking to the average Athenian) could be brought up against him to make a charge of 'impiety' plausible. He fled to the Spartans, frightened them with an account of Athens' far-reaching designs, and induced the Peloponnesians to send volunteers and a Spartan general to Sicily and to recommence the war at home.

The Athenian expedition was besieging Syracuse, whose citizen soldiers were at first no match for the war-hardened Athenians; but they defended themselves with doggedness and resource; in this Dorian democracy the Athenians, says Thucydides, found opponents all too like themselves. When Syracuse was reinforced, the besiegers found their own communications cut; and finally the whole expedition, reinforced from Athens, was almost

Ill. 109

106, 107 An Athenian memorial of the Pylos victory and the lost opportunity to make peace. *Right*, the inscription: 'THE ATHENIANS [dedicated these spoils taken] FROM THE SPARTANS AT PYLOS'; *far left*, the shield (crushed, and lacking its leather backing) as it is today. Although in fact the Spartans on Sphakteria island had been overwhelmed only by numbers, it was a proud day for Athens when she could dedicate these spoils from Spartans actually forced to surrender

108 Going to the wars. The farewell scene in which a hoplite takes leave of his father or wife is a frequent motif in the art of this warlike age. Note the leather attachment hanging from the shield to protect the legs, a comparatively rare feature

wholly lost; 175 ships and nearly 40,000 men of Athens and her allies (413 BC).

Even then Athens did not collapse. With Ionia in revolt, the Dardanelles and Bosporus disputed, and a Spartan fortress (recommended by Alcibiades) ten miles from her walls, she built new ships and fought on for nine more years. Twice she won great naval victories, and rejected peace terms that did not restore her Empire. At last, indiscipline and the cunning of the grim and able Spartan admiral, Lysander, led to her last great fleet being surprised ashore at the Aegospotami ('Goat-Rivers') in the Dardanelles. Even then, she stood a siege. The war ended with Athens starving. Even her democracy was suppressed; but the group of aristocrats (some of them, also, friends of Socrates) whom Sparta installed as a provisional government, soon made themselves so unpopular (the 'Thirty Tyrants') that the people rose to restore the democracy (403); and a Spartan king had the

Ill. 108

wisdom to let it be. At the fort of Phyle, ten miles north of Athens, where the democrats made their first stand, later Athenian walls may still be seen.

The End of the Golden Age

Sparta had inherited Athens' power, and kept her own; but she failed to bring unity, more disastrously and more quickly than Athens. Her military governors proved both arrogant and full of greed for money, of which the Laws of Lycurgus deprived them at home. Sparta had gone into alliance with Persia, to finance her late naval operations; then, inheriting Athens' position in Ionia, she found herself at war with Persia; but Persia found no difficulty in using her money to finance Sparta's enemies. Within ten years of the fall of Athens, Athens herself, Thebes Argos and Corinth were in alliance against Sparta. With Persian money Conon, an Athenian admiral who had escaped from Aegospotami, rebuilt the fortifications of Piraeus. The allies were bloodily defeated before Corinth in 394; but Sparta had to recall her king and army from Asia, and in a new general peace settlement (387) she abandoned the Greeks of Asia to Persian rule. The divisions of the Greeks had undone the work of 479.

Ill. 111

The fourth century BC is the age of Late Classical art, of Plato and Aristotle and of the great orators, who incidentally give, in their law-court speeches, many vivid pictures of Athenian life; but in political history, it reveals the moral bankruptcy of the city-state world. There is no lack of colourful personalities; one of the greatest was Dionysius, tyrant of Syracuse from 405 to his death in 367. He rose to power through faction in the Syracusan democracy, and after a Carthaginian army, reversing the verdict of 480, had sacked Himera and Selinus. His four Carthaginian wars, punctuated by wars of aggression against the Greeks of Italy, where he plundered Rhegium and Croton, left Carthage still in possession of a third of

109 Many of the finest coins of mature Greek numismatic art are the work of late fifth- and of fourth-century artists. Syracuse, in the pride of her defeat of the great Athenian expedition, as after the victory over Carthage in 480, once more struck ten-drachma pieces. Once more we see the head of Arethusa surrounded by dolphins, once more, on the reverse, the chariot, with Winged Victory crowning the charioteer; and it is interesting to study the change of style in sixty-six years, in the treatment of identical subjects (*cf. Ill. 85*). A new feature is the display of captured Athenian arms in the exergue (a separate field, reverse, bottom) with the legend, visible on some specimens, 'ATHLA' ('spoils')

Sicily, and a trail of devastation. In the meantime Dionysius also wrote tragedies for exhibition at Athens; he fell sick and died after a feast to celebrate his being at last awarded the first prize. He was by then the most powerful man in the Greek world, and had sent troops to intervene in the wars of old Greece.

110 Chalcidian League tetradrachms, with Apollo's head and lyre, and legend 'CHALKIDEON', are much admired – and also sometimes forged

The centres of power in the Greek world were tending to move outwards. Greek civilization, like that of western Christendom after it, developed first in the relative isolation of a peninsula and its neighbouring islands, whence pressure of population had led to colonization overseas; later, as the political arts and technology of the developing civilization spread outwards, not only colonial areas, but adjacent continental countries, formerly backward and thinly populated, grow in power; in the Greek world, Sicily and Chalcidice, then Macedonia and lastly Rome. In Chalcidice Olynthus formed a confederacy of cities, with which Amyntas, King of Macedonia, made

111 The Ceramicus (Kerameikos, 'Potters' Quarter') near the western Dipylon Gate of Athens. The tombstone with a cavalryman commemorates Dexileos, a 'war hero' killed at Corinth in 394 (p. 112)

112 The shapely and well-preserved fourth-century towers of Athens' frontier fort (Eleuthérai?) near the crest of the pass on the shortest road to Thebes

alliance; for a time it even included the Macedonian city of Pella. But Sparta looked with jealousy upon this rising power and, on the pretext of defending the liberties of cities which did not wish to join, demolished the Chalcidian League in a war (382–379). While a Spartan officer with troops for this was passing through Boeotia, a Theban political faction offered to put the citadel of Thebes into his hands. He accepted the offer, and by this act of treachery Sparta, through her friends, dominated Thebes; it was the culminating-point of Sparta's power.

But a Theban band, operating from Athenian territory, liberated their city after three years; and in the war that followed it became evident that Sparta, with a disastrously falling birthrate and shrinking Spartiate aristocracy, was loath to risk the losses of a pitched battle. Thebes produced a great soldier and statesman, Epaminondas; and when at last a Spartan king gave battle in Boeotia, with superior numbers and an apparently won position, Epaminondas broke through the Spartans' own ranks with a charge by a dense column, and the Spartans' allies at once withdrew. Four hundred Spartiates, more than

half those present and a third of all those between eighteen and sixty, fell with their king on this Flodden Field of the Spartan aristocracy, the Battle of Leuctra, 371.

Epaminondas invaded the Peloponnese; he liberated Messenia, where the new walls of Messene, in the great amphitheatre of Mount Ithome, remain as the finest of all examples of classical Greek fortification. He encouraged the Arcadians to develop federal institutions, and weakened Sparta for ever. (As a natural sequel, we then soon find Athens and Sparta allied against Thebes.) But agrarian Thebes possessed even less than Sparta the economic potential to succeed where Athens had failed; nor could she replace Epaminondas when he fell in battle against Athenians and Spartans, with allies on both sides, at Mantinea in Arcadia (362). Within ten years, Thebes was finding herself baffled in a war even with her neighbours, the men of Phocis, who, under pressure, 'borrowed' and then more and more unblushingly spent the treasures of Delphi, to hire mercenaries. The Boeotians sought for allies in their 'Sacred War' against impious Phocis. They found a very effective one in Philip, King of Macedonia.

Ill. 112

CHAPTER SIX

The Rise of Macedon

Philip, as a boy, had been carried off to Thebes as a hostage; so far was his country from being then a world-power. In the city of Epaminondas he learned to admire Greek culture, and studied the Theban army. At twenty-two he became king (359), when his elder brother was defeated and killed by the Illyrians. Reorganizing his army and promoting in it a great general, Parmenio, he next year dealt the Illyrians a shattering blow; but he was still surrounded by enemies. He triumphed over them not only by personally leading his troops – he was repeatedly wounded – but by consummate, Machiavellian diplomacy; buying off enemies till he could deal with them one at a time, winning men by the charm of his personality, lavish of gifts to ambassadors and politicians, and of promises, which he kept no longer than suited him, to all and sundry. He made his way less by deceiving the innocent (the Greeks were no innocents) than by playing on the cupidity and ambition of men who matched him in unscrupulousness, but not in intellect. Thus, he dissuaded the Athenians from helping Amphipolis, an Athenian colony liberated long since by Brasidas, by making a secret offer to Athenian generals in the north Aegean to trade it for Pydna, a Greek town on the Macedonian coast, which was in alliance with Athens.

Ill. 113

113 Silver tetradrachm of Philip of Macedonia (reverse) with the horseman that both punned on Philip's name ('Lover of horses') and commemorated the prowess of the Macedonian cavalry

114 Demosthenes: one of the better ancient busts that show the grim features of this stern 'water-drinker' (as his enemies said) whose Churchillian oratory scourged the easygoing Athenian democracy into war with Philip

This very dirty deal by the Athenians was suitably paid for when Philip's troops were admitted to Pydna by friends within, and he kept both towns. Soon after he took Potidaea, which Athens also coveted, and presented it to Olynthus, thus ensuring that, at least for the present, Athens and Olynthus would not make common cause against him.

Athens, since 378, had been trying to re-form her naval league, with safeguards against using it as an instrument of imperialism; but her allies never fully trusted her. The case of Pydna shows how right they were. In 357, for reasons unconnected with Pydna, four of the largest cities, Chios, Cos, Rhodes and Byzantium seceded; Athens failed to coerce them by force, and was left with only a few rags of her League; while Philip defeated inland tribes and secured his hold on the Pangaean gold-mines, where he founded Philippi.

Philip and the Phocians first clashed in faction-ridden Thessaly, where Philip, after sustaining two defeats, drove a Phocian army into the sea near modern Volos; but the Athenians kept him out of Phocis by holding Thermopylae; Philip, ever a realist, did not attack (352). His next conquests were in Thrace; then in Chalcidice, where Athens, whipped up by the fierce oratory of Demosthenes, aided Olynthus – but too little and too late. Philip razed the city and annexed the area (348). Athens treated for peace; but the negotiations were long drawn, and actually during them Philip marched past unguarded Thermopylae and reduced Phocis to total submission, while its leaders and their mercenaries fled abroad. He was welcomed at Delphi as a liberator and victorious crusader (346). He was master of northern Greece, and popular with the aristocracy in Thessaly, whom he had helped by overthrowing a tyrant of the commercial town of Pherae (near modern Volos). Next he completed the conquest of Thrace. He was repulsed from

Ill. 114

115 Alexander, youthful and ferocious, leads the charge against Darius' centre at Issus. Detail from the vast 'Issus' mosaic from Pompeii, reproducing probably a Greek painting of about 300 BC. Greek painting, owing to the perishable character of the materials, has almost entirely disappeared; but the more durable medium of mosaic gives us the means to appreciate the methods and especially the power of composition of the school of Alexander's court painter, Apelles

Perinthus, on the Sea of Marmara, and Byzantium, with help both from Persia and Athens (340); but in the same year another quarrel at Delphi gave him an excuse for intervening again in Central Greece. Thebes was directly threatened. Towards Athens, Philip protested feelings of respect and a desire for friendship, probably quite sincerely; but in the name of Hellas, Demosthenes successfully urged an alliance with Thebes. In the hard-fought Battle of Chaeronea, in 338, Philip beat the united armies of Central Greece. His eighteen-year-old son, Alexander, led the decisive cavalry charge. Philip then garrisoned Thebes, but even now did not invade Attica, and gave Athens peace on easy terms.

Ill. 118

His ambition was by no means satisfied. He was still only forty-three, and moreover he was not in a position to draw rein; for his armies, with a large professional or mercenary component, were so expensive that, for all his Thracian gold, he was in debt. Only the spoils of Asia

116 Opposite to Alexander, the 'Issus' mosaic shows Darius, terrified, in the act of descending from his high chariot, to flee from the field on horseback. The viewpoint selected by the artist is from just behind the Persian king's 'command vehicle'. Alexander, leading the cavalry of his right wing, storms in from the left, while the back of the scene is dominated by a menacing line of spears: the upraised pikes of the rear ranks of the Macedonian phalanx, attacking frontally

17 Alexander and Roxane. This splendid cameo in Vienna shows the idealized portraits of the king and his Persian bride, daughter of a Bactrian baron who had surrendered after a brave resistance. She was the mother of his only child (p. 125), a posthumous son, also called Alexander, who perished with his mother, murdered during the struggles between the generals, while still a child

118 The Lion of Chaeronea. Rebuilt from fragments, this monument to the Greeks killed in battle against Philip and Alexander in 338 stands facing the road into Boeotia from the north-west. Athenians, Boeotians and Achaians were among those who took part in this dour stand for freedom. This gateway into Central Greece from the north, along the plain of the Boeotian Cephisus, between rugged hills on either side, was the scene of so many great battles that Greeks sometimes referred to Boeotia as 'the Dancing-Floor of Ares'; in our less poetic equivalent, the 'cockpit of Greece'

could make his style of conquest pay; and Greeks had been telling each other, ever since the Ten Thousand with Xenophon had marched home from Mesopotamia, how weak Persia had become, and how easy it would be to conquer her if Greeks could only stop fighting each other. At Corinth, where the Greek General Headquarters had been in Xerxes' time, Philip called a national congress; it elected him Captain-General of the Greeks for a great war of righteous revenge; and in 336 Parmenio crossed the Dardanelles to make good a bridgehead.

But it was not Philip who was to conduct that enterprise. Promiscuous in his habits, he had long been on bad terms with his Queen, the fiery Olympias; and in 337 he had married the niece of one of his generals, who, at the wedding, prayed for the birth of 'a legitimate heir', an open attack on Alexander's position. In 336 a son was born to him; and soon after that, Philip was murdered at a festival. The assassin, a young man with a private grievance, was killed by the guards; and who might have encouraged him remained always, at least officially, unknown.

119 Greek or Macedonian attacking a Persian: a detail from the 'Alexander sarcophagus', from Sidon. In high relief, decorated with paint, which survives though faded, and even provided with metal swords, spears and horse-harness, these figures are highly naturalistic and, up to a point, 'documentary'; though some details, such as the nakedness of the Greek in this scene, derive from Greek artistic convention

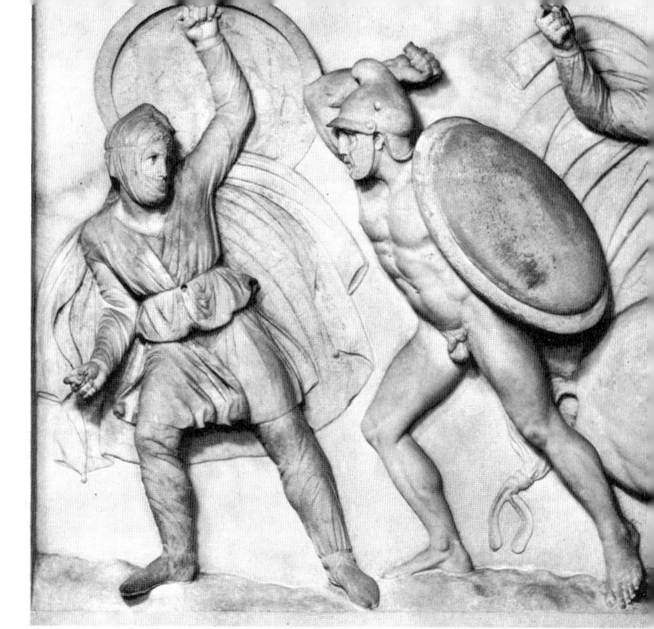

World Empire

Alexander, a king at twenty, was at once faced by rebellion on all sides; but he quickly showed his astonishing quality as a general. A swift march, merely to show himself in Greece – cutting steps in the side of Ossa when the Thessalian government demurred at letting him through the Tempe Gorge – averted trouble there and then; but in 335 he fought three critical campaigns. He swept through Thrace, storming the Shipka Pass and crossing the Danube, where he had an interview with fair-haired Celts on the move; across into Illyria, where he was trapped, it seemed, in the hills, and extricated himself with typical daring and cunning; and down again into Greece, where Thebes had risen and was besieging the Macedonians in the citadel. He razed the city to the ground; and Greece was cowed.

Then, in 334, he crossed into Asia, demolished the army of the local Satraps after a fierce cavalry mêlée, and liberated Ionia. In 333 he defeated King Darius at Issus in Syria. Half the next year was occupied by a desperate siege of Tyre; necessary, because the Phoenician fleet,

Ills 115, 116

120 The map shows better than words the vast extent of country through which Alexander and his 40,000–45,000 fighting men carved their way. The thousands of Greek mercenaries who joined him were used largely for garrisons, while his Macedonian striking force was maintained by drafts

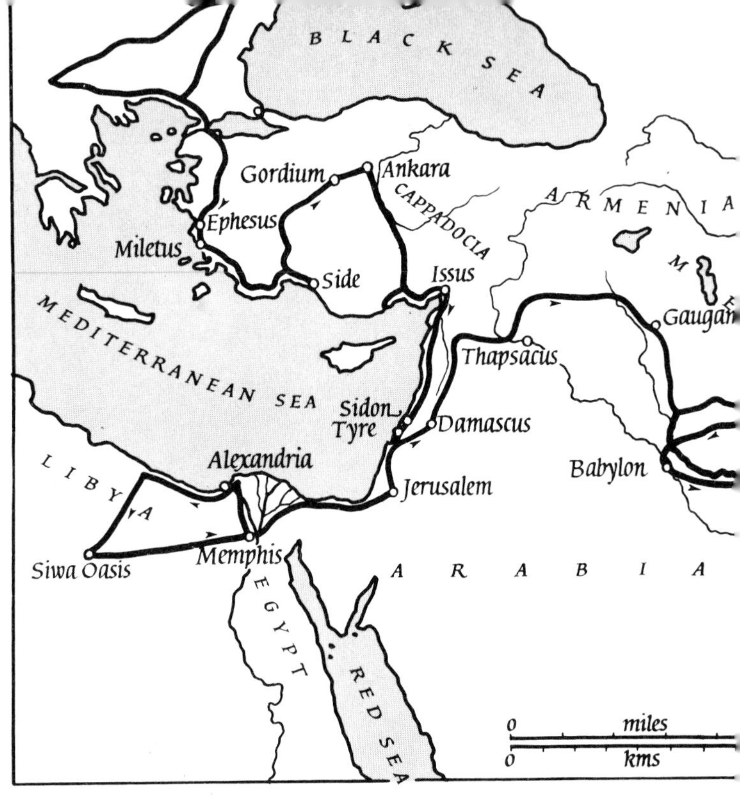

121, 122 Coins of Alexander, wearing, *above*, the lion's skin of his ancestor Heracles; and *below* an elephant head-dress, symbolic of his Indian conquests

with Greek mercenaries and enterprising Persian commanders, was still at large, trying to raise Greece in revolt in his rear. By the year's end, Phoenicia had fallen, and he was in Egypt. In 331 he fought his greatest battle at Gaugamela, in open country (unlike Issus) east of the Tigris. Vastly outnumbered, he stalled off enveloping attacks with flank-guards until his infantry phalanx and heavy horse-guards could smash the enemy centre and drive Darius once more in flight. Darius retired eastward, on Ecbatana; Alexander rested in Babylon awhile, letting rumours spread that his army was demoralized by its vices, and then marched out *south*-east, fighting his way in midwinter through mountain chains, first against tribesmen, then against the home levy of Persia proper, to occupy Persepolis, the ancient capital, to destroy its palaces and, more important, to round up its young men and send them afar, to be trained by Macedonian officers as soldiers of the new king.

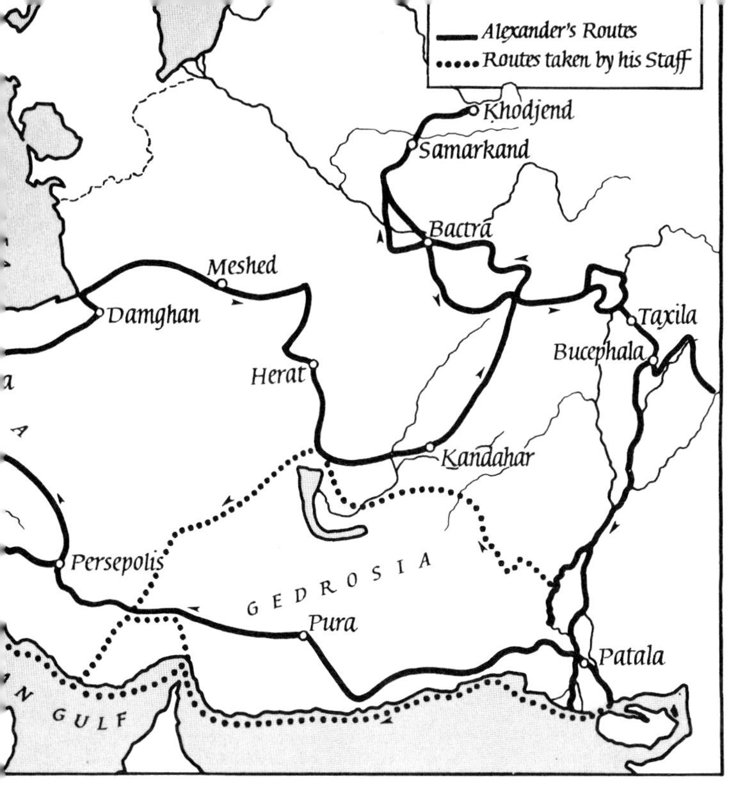

By this tremendous exploitation of victory, Darius was left with no army in 330, except the forces of his eastern barons; and they, in retreat from Ecbatana, put him under arrest and, when Alexander's pursuit grew hot, murdered him. But Alexander's conquest of the Empire was but half done. Three years of strenuous warfare were needed to subdue the tough eastern frontier provinces, where castle after mountain castle stood a siege, and conquered provinces rose again in his rear. Unwearied still, by 326 he was conquering the Punjab; and there at last his Macedonians refused to go further. They had won a very severe battle against the Paurava rajah (the 'Poros' of western writers), who had two hundred elephants; and they declined to march against the Ganges kingdoms, which were reported to have five thousand. In 325 Alexander returned to Babylon, after nearly perishing along with a column which he led to explore the desert coast of the Persian Gulf.

Ill. 120

Ill. 123

Alexander's character has been disputed to this day. There had been more than one conspiracy against him; one of them had been at least concealed by Philotas, son of Parmenio, general of the horse-guards, when it was reported to him – perhaps out of envy, combined with indignation that Parmenio had been left behind on base duties at Ecbatana. Philotas was put to death; and immediately thereafter Parmenio was murdered, as an inevitable preventive measure. Callisthenes, the official historian, nephew of Alexander's boyhood tutor, Aristotle, perished after a conspiracy among the royal pages, to whom Callisthenes taught history – and had talked of tyrants and tyrannicide. Alexander himself had killed, in a drinking-party, his foster-brother Clitus, who had saved his life in the first cavalry battle, but who now drunkenly provoked him, complaining of his use of Persian dress and Persian despotic ways, and assumption of glory that belonged to all the army; the act cost the King an agony of remorse. Considering the strain under which he lived, these tragedies, though grim, are not numerous; but they made enemies. Certainly Alexander had a constructive side. He founded many cities; some, such as Herat and Khodjend ('Alexandria-at-the-World's-End'), were Greek re-foundations of existing towns; but the greatest, Alexandria in Egypt, was new. He set out deliberately to employ Persian officers and governors (some failed him, and had to be replaced by Macedonians) and to equalize the two master-races; a policy which his Macedonians bitterly resented. But by personally leading them in charge and escalade, repeatedly wounded, once almost to death; by sharing their hardships, by efficiency, glamour and success, he kept their loyalty, with rare outbreaks of exasperation, to the end.

On the other hand, a serious count against him is the fact that, while continually risking his life, he made no arrangement whatever for the rule of his empire or the

123 Alexander's Indian victories are still more explicitly commemorated on the reverse of this large ten-drachma piece. Like most such large pieces in Greek coinage, it is a victory issue. The victory over the elephants of the Paurava king is represented by the Macedonian horseman with his long lance, who pursues and thrusts at an Indian, retreating on his elephant, as 'Poros' himself, after a brave resistance, was said to have done. The elephant devices on Alexander's coins also herald the important part that elephants were to play on the battlefields of the following century

command of the army when he should be gone. He did not even beget a son until the last year of his short life (by the Persian princess Roxane); though Parmenio and others begged him to leave an heir to Macedonia before plunging into Asia. Nor, though passionate in friendship, does he seem to have been homosexual. It looks indeed as though his beloved mother's comments on his father's infidelities had imbued him from childhood with an abnormal disgust with sex. All his energy was poured into war and government. The theory that, had he lived, he would have renounced war, cannot be sustained. He was organizing a large new army, two-thirds Medo-Persian, one-third Macedonian, when, not yet thirty-three, he caught a fever and died (323).

Ill. 117

CHAPTER SEVEN

After Alexander

124, 125 Coins of Alexander's successors give genuine portraits of these tough and not uncultivated men. *Above*, Seleucus I; *below*, Ptolemy I, with royal diadem

The 'Fetters of Greece'

So Alexander died, 'intestate'; and after years of warfare between his generals, the empire he left was divided between those who survived. Seleucus, last commander of Alexander's foot-guards, won most of it, in Asia. Egypt was secured by the far-sighted Ptolemy; he founded a dynasty that ended only with Cleopatra in 31 BC. It was a purely Greco-Macedonian state (its higher civilian officials Greek, its army officers mostly Greek or Macedonian), administering the hard-worked fellahin through an elaborate bureaucracy; its intellectual glory was the royal Temple of the Muses at Alexandria, with its great library and the salaried scholars who worked there. Cleopatra is said to have been the first of her line ever to learn Egyptian. Macedonia, after being overrun by Celts from Central Europe, whom, as we saw, Alexander had met on the Danube, and who penetrated to Delphi during the years of confusion, was restored as a nation-state by Antigonus, grandson of one of the marshals of the same name, and of Antipater, who had governed Macedonia for Alexander; his dynasty, which lasted until the Roman conquest in 168, controlled Greece through garrisons at strategic points: Demetrias – near modern

126 The 'Fetters of Greece', as these strongholds were called prevented anti-Macedonian forces from getting together. Demetrias watched the routes between Thessaly and the south; Chalcis blocked the strategically important sheltered sea-ways; Corinth held the Isthmus and when Athens rose in 264–262, a king of Sparta was killed trying to force the Isthmus lines and come to her rescue. There was also a garrison in Piraeus and at the Hill of the Muses (head of the Long Walls), until 229, when Athens, while Macedonia was in trouble with northern barbarians, bought her freedom and proclaimed her neutrality

Volos – Chalcis, Piraeus and Corinth; they were called 'the Fetters of Greece'.

Greece, though her states were dwarfed by the new giant kingdoms, was still important as a source of trained manpower: soldiers, philosophers, poets (a royal prestige-symbol) and technicians. As in a later Europe, there was some attempt by the states to draw together; the federal Achaean League, including also part of Arcadia, and the Aetolian League in the north-west, were the two chief power-blocs, and by no means the least interesting of Greek political experiments; but unfortunately, as rivals, they were always hostile to each other. Athens, after a gallant attempt to throw off Macedonian supremacy with help from Egypt (which let her down), became more and more a 'university city'; but Sparta, strengthened under King Cleomenes III by a redistribution of land and emancipation of some helots – Sparta's revolution, three hundred years too late – emerged once more to alarm a

Ills 127, 128

127, 128 These coins, though dating from before the Macedonian supremacy (both *c.* 370–360), illustrate the development of local federal institutions. *Above*, a coin of the Achaean League (then still confined to its coastal strip) with the head of Apollo and, on the reverse, the seated figure of Zeus, with legend 'ACHAION'; *below*, a coin of the Arcadian League as reorganized by Epaminondas (p. 115) with the head of Zeus and on the reverse, Pan, originally an Arcadian deity

world in which the rich were too rich and the poor too many; only to go down before Macedonians and Achaeans, scared into common action, in the Battle of Sellasia, six miles north of Sparta, in 221.

The Greeks in the East

In Asia the House of Seleucus, claiming the whole of the old Persian Empire from the Aegean to Afghanistan, faced an impossible task; the kings grappled manfully with it for two hundred years. Seleucus himself ceded the Punjab to the great Indian, Chandragupta, for five hundred trained elephants, which he used to crush his rival, the elder Antigonus, in Asia Minor. The kings, themselves descended from Persian noblemen through Seleucus' Persian wife, made some use of Iranian officers; but Greco-Macedonian jealousy set limits to that wise policy, and of Greeks and Macedonians themselves they could never get enough, though they encouraged colonization and recruited what they could, in rivalry with Macedonia and the Ptolemies. Thus lacking an imperial *nation*, the huge state was continually shrinking.

Ill. 129

129 Coin of Seleucus (*cf. Ill. 124*); elephant and legend, 'OF KING SELEUKOS'. The Successors, at first professing to be viceroys for Alexander's infant son and weak-minded half-brother, assume the royal title after their murder

130–132 Barely known or in some cases not at all from literary history, these kings of the east come vividly before us in their magnificent coin-portraits. Antimachus of Bactria (*above*) and Eucratides, on the largest ancient gold coin extant, (*right*) shield their heads with broad-brimmed sun-hat and sun-helmet; Menander the Just in India (*below*) still wears the simple diadem of a Macedonian king

In Asia Minor the Celts, ferried over from Europe (278) by a local chief who hoped to use them for his own ends, proceeded to terrorise the whole land. Antiochus I, the son of Seleucus, with elephants in his army, beat them back from the east; but they remained in the region called after them, Galatia. Ionia was delivered from their raids by resistance organized chiefly by the lords of Pergamum (kings, after *c.* 240), who were enabled by the rivalries of the greater powers to found a state of their own. The sculptures of Pergamum, celebrating in florid style their defeats of the Gauls, are famous; their library was second only to that of Alexandria. Native kingdoms with some tincture of Greek sculpture (Bithynia and Pontus) divided the Black Sea coast; while the Seleucids kept open little more than a route to the Aegean, between Galatia and the Taurus Mountains.

While Seleucids and Ptolemies squandered their resources in fighting for Syria, Iran went out of control. Diodotus, Governor of Bactria, the north-east frontier region, where Alexander had settled many of his Greek mercenaries, proclaimed himself king (*c.* 255?); his

Ills 130–132

successors had some of the most splendid of Greek coins struck for them. Further west, where there were few Greek troops, a nomad tribe settled in the old province of Parthia, killed its Greek governor, and founded a kingdom, weak at first, but later powerful. Seleucid attempts at reconquest failed, largely for lack of troops to occupy the vast territories. Antiochus III (223–187), the last powerful Seleucid, marched to the Oxus and reasserted his suzerainty over both kingdoms; but it lapsed after he had come to grief in the west against the rising power of Rome (see p. 134). The Greeks of Bactria then embarked on a remarkable adventure. Their king Demetrius reconquered the Punjab – he is the 'great Emetrius, Lord of Ind', known to Chaucer. But behind his back one Eucratides, perhaps nominally acting for the Seleucids, seized power in Bactria itself; so Greek manpower was once more divided. Nevertheless, the Indo-Greek kings displayed great vigour, even reaching the Ganges. One of them, Menander the Just (*c.* 150 BC?), is the 'Milinda' of a famous Buddhist dialogue. Soon after this, Bactria was overrun by the Central Asian nomads. Greek India, further subdivided among rival generals and increasingly Indianized, as its later coins show, may have lasted another century before suffering the same fate. Meanwhile, the Arsakid kings of Parthia, less spectacular, but nearer to their subjects in speech and culture, and at the same time quite willing to strike coins with Greek legends (often including the word 'phil-hellene'), survived and prospered. By 130 they had finally won Mesopotamia from the Seleucids. Then, for three hundred years, though sometimes defeated, they held their ground against Rome.

133 Demetrius of India, diademed here, on some other coins wears an elephant head-dress like that of Alexander (*Ill. 122*); but whatever he wore, he clearly did not demand artistic flattery

CHAPTER EIGHT

The Shadow of Rome

We must turn to record the onward march of that western giant that was to put an end to the warring states of Greece and ultimately to give the land three hundred years of peace (*c.* 30 BC – AD 270).

Already in the fifth century Italian tribes, increasingly well armed, had begun to cut short the borders of the Greek colonies. Cumae fell to the Samnites about 420, surviving with a mixed population and a dull and provincial culture, and now outgrown by the adjacent 'New Town', Naples. Poseidonia (Paestum) followed; Thurii sustained a bloody defeat by the Lucanians in 390, and the southern cities were further weakened by a temporary conquest by Dionysius of Syracuse (p. 112). Later in the century, Taranto, which in her secluded position now remained the strongest colony, repeatedly asked for help from the old country. Two kings of Sparta, which still kept her military skill and prestige, campaigned in Italy (*c.* 338 and 303) and between them (334–330) a king of Epirus, Alexander, uncle and brother-in-law of Alexander the Great. What was fatal to these enterprises was the old Greek *philótimon*; the kings dreamed of carving out an empire for themselves, and their allies consequently turned against them. In 282 Thurii, having had experience of Taranto's friends, appealed for protection, not to her but to Rome, the more civilized city which had defeated the Samnite hill-men in long wars and was now mistress of a confederacy embracing all central Italy. This led to war with Taranto, which had an old treaty with Rome and objected to the Roman presence in her 'sphere of influence'; and Taranto called in another king of Epirus, the famous Pyrrhus.

This was Rome's first Greek war. She sustained two bloody defeats, but won through by dogged courage and because, while Rome could replace losses almost indefinitely out of a manpower running into hundreds of thousands, Pyrrhus could not. He returned to Greece, to be killed in a war with Antigonus Gonatas in 272; and his garrison in Taranto, which he had recalled, surrendered the city to the Romans to secure an undisturbed withdrawal.

Greek Sicily fell during Rome's wars with Carthage. After the first (264–241) Rome took over most of the island as a province. Repeatedly fought over and ravaged – the beautiful city of Acragas (Agrigento), the second largest in the island, had been twice sacked and once burnt – Sicily under the Romans was chiefly a source of grain, grown on large, slave-run farms. Syracuse and the south-east survived under the last of the city's great soldier-kings, Hiero (270–216), who had been Rome's ally. Excavations of country-town houses show, in Sicily as in the Hellenistic east, a level of middle-class comfort that had never been higher. Hiero missed his chance of patronizing Theocritus, the creator of pastoral poetry, who emigrated, a disappointed man, to win greater success in Egypt; but he had a great subject in Archimedes, the engineer and mathematician, discoverer of the principle of specific gravity, who returned from Alexandria to his native city. But when Hiero died, old and honoured, Rome's Second Punic (*i.e.* Phoenician) War had broken out; Hannibal was in Italy and had won his early sensational victories. The Syracusan leaders thought the time ripe to change sides; but they were wrong, and in 212 the city was sacked by M. Claudius Marcellus. Archimedes was killed, unrecognized, by a Roman soldier. Marcellus, a man of some culture who had given orders to save Archimedes, also pillaged Syracuse of its works of art, starting a Roman practice that went on for centuries.

In Greece meanwhile a supreme attempt had been made to put an end to the wars. In 217 a peace conference was held at Naupactus (Lepanto). Philip V, the brilliant young king of Macedonia, was there in person. Agelaus of Naupactus, welcoming the delegates, pointed to the giant struggle proceeding in Italy. Now, he said, was the time when Greeks must hold hands like men wading through a violent torrent: 'for if the cloud now rising in the west should spread to Greece, I fear we shall be praying the gods to give us back the chance to call even our quarrels our own'. Everyone applauded, and a peace was indeed made, but then Philip made a fatal error. After Hannibal's crowning victory at Cannae (216), he thought, like the Sicilians, that Rome was falling; and in 215 Macedonia came into the war on Hannibal's side. Philip had failed to appreciate both Rome's vast reserves of manpower, and the fact that during the First Punic War she had become much the strongest *naval* power in the world. In 214 a modest Roman force landed at Apollonia, near modern Valona. In 212 Rome secured the alliance of the Aetolians; and for several years desultory hostilities proceeded. They had little effect on the course of the great war; but Philip's action had drawn Roman forces for the first time into Greece.

In 205, when Carthage was clearly failing, peace was made. But Rome, after so much blood shed in repelling invasions from oversea, had grown, like Russia, genuinely though needlessly afraid of being attacked again. The Senate in 201, immediately after the surrender of Carthage, with difficulty persuaded the people that if they did not

134 T. Quinctius Flamininus, from a gold coin struck out of the spoils of victory after 196 BC. It is noteworthy that Roman Republican magistrates now put their heads on coins like Hellenistic kings

fight Philip in Greece they would have to do so in Italy. Their excuse was Philip's aggression in the Aegean against the naval state of Rhodes and the King of Pergamum, who had treaties with Rome. Volunteer legions were raised, and after three indecisive campaigns the Romans and Aetolians broke Philip's main army at Cynoscephalae in Thessaly. Philip was forced to become Rome's ally and to withdraw all garrisons from Greece; and after defeating his ally, Sparta, where the revolution had broken out again under a fierce terrorist, Nabis, the young Roman commander Flamininus announced at Corinth, amid scenes of wild enthusiasm, the withdrawal of Roman garrisons, too. Greece was to be free.

Almost inevitably, it did not work. The Aetolians, prevented from extending their own power, invited the great Seleucid, Antiochus III, to 'liberate' Greece from the Roman settlement; and Rome's raw nerve was touched again. A Roman army from the north destroyed the king's advance corps at Thermopylae after storming the hills inland, and in 190 his main army was routed in Asia Minor and he was deprived of all territory west of the Taurus, to the temporary advantage of Pergamum. It was the first Roman operation in Asia. Macedonia was destroyed in a third war (168), after complaints of its alleged aggressive designs from Pergamum, and broken up into four republics; its last king, Perseus, died interned in Italy. The Aetolian League was then dissolved into its component villages, after hundreds of nationalists there had been massacred by their enemies, backed by Roman troops. Epirus was depopulated in a huge slave-making operation, carried out with cold-blooded treachery after surrender, in order to provide Roman troops with a money-bonus. A thousand Achaeans, chiefly democrats, were carried off to Italy 'for trial' – and then kept for fifteen years, during which time seven hundred of them died. Finally the Achaean League, its leaders continually reported on to Rome by their opponents, and now prevented from coercing Sparta, which had been forced to join it, took up arms in a hopeless war and was destroyed. Corinth, its greatest city, was razed to the ground and its whole population sold into slavery in 146; the same year in which Carthage, likewise goaded into a desperate resistance, suffered the same fate. It is of Corinth that the story is told how the consul Mummius, when consigning shiploads of Old Masters to Rome, insisted on the routine clause in his contract with the shippers, that if any of these items were lost or damaged they should be replaced by others as good.

The sad story of the end of Greek freedom is told for us best by Polybius, the third great master among Greek historians. Son of a general of the Achaean League, he was among the thousand carried off in 167, and was fortunate enough to be taken into the home of Aemilius, the conqueror of Macedonia. He became a close friend of Aemilius' son, later, by adoption, a Scipio, and famous as the destroyer of Carthage: Scipio Africanus II. Polybius saw Carthage burn, and Scipio weep. He saw Corinth burn, and was able at least to mediate on behalf of his countrymen in the smaller cities. But the League was dissolved, and war forbidden. So Greece *did* lose the power 'to call even her quarrels her own'. Ironically, she received through foreign conquest the peace that her own brilliant and turbulent children had never managed to maintain. Polybius had lived through the history which he describes, and, knowing many of the best Romans, sincerely believed that these were men fit to give peace to the world. A thorough Greek, he could hate some of his fellow countrymen with the worst, but he is sincere and intelligent. He had hoped passionately, when he wrote his earlier books, that the worst, as seen at Corinth, might be avoided; and we must heed him when he infers sadly that Greeks had brought it upon themselves.

135 Head of Pompey, the first great Roman organizer of the Greek east, by a Greek artist

Roman penetration of the eastern kingdoms was already advancing. The Roman Senate, dominated by great landowners, corporately did not want oversea commitments. But with vast amounts of gold and silver flowing into Rome as tribute or plain loot, and seeking investment, Italian merchants, slave-traders and money-lenders, including agents for rich senators, were everywhere. So the Roman government was drawn in to protect its nationals, both against the hatred of debtors and against piracy, which developed when Rome had demolished other sea-powers and ceased to maintain her own. Attalus III of Pergamum, having no direct heir, actually left his kingdom by will to the Roman People, to become the Province of Asia (133); but any hopes he may have cherished of securing a satisfactory future for it were doomed, for it became a pawn in Roman politics and was subjected to an appalling system of tax-farming. Great syndicates at Rome bid for the privilege of collecting the taxes, and set out to collect as much more as they could. After a generation of this, when King Mithradates of Pontus, whose kingdom was next in line for penetration, struck back at Rome during a civil war in Italy, eighty thousand Italian men, women and children in Asia are said to have been massacred (88 BC). Mithradates crossed to Greece, and when Sulla drove his generals out Piraeus was destroyed and Athens plundered but spared. The Seleucid kingdom, reduced to Syria and there weakened by the Jewish rebellion of the Maccabees, which Rome encouraged, was finally extinguished during these wars by the Iranian King of Armenia; and Pompey, the general who made an end of Mithradates and of the pirate menace, then constituted the provinces of Syria and Bithynia, settling the map of Western Asia that was to last for centuries. The Ptolemies in Egypt survived various vicissitudes until the fall of Cleopatra at the end of the Roman civil wars.

136 Coin of Cleopatra. The candid likeness, characteristic of Hellenistic coinage, suggests that exceptional beauty was not among Cleopatra's advantages, and the length of her nose not a major factor in world-history

Bibliography

NDREWES, A. *The Greek Tyrants*, London, 1954.
— *The Greeks*, London, 1967.
RRIAN *The Life of Alexander the Great*, trs. A. de Sélincourt, Harmondsworth, 1968.
ALDRY, H. C. *Ancient Greek Literature in its Living Context*, London, 1968.
OARDMAN, J. *Greek Art*, London, 1964.
— *The Greeks Overseas*, Harmondsworth, 1964.
OWRA, C. M. *The Greek Experience*, London, 1957.
URN, A. R. *Alexander the Great and the Hellenistic Empire*, London, 1947.
— *Pericles and Athens*, London, 1948.
— *The Lyric Age of Greece*, London, 1960.
— *Persia and the Greeks*, London, 1962.
— *The Pelican History of Greece*, Harmondsworth, 1966.
URY, J. B. *A History of Greece to the Death of Alexander the Great*, 3rd ed., London, 1951.
ARY, M. A. *A History of the Greek World from 323 to 146 BC*, London, 1932.
HRENBERG, V. *From Solon to Socrates*, London, 1968.
ORREST, W. G. *The Emergence of Greek Democracy*, London, 1966.
ROTE, G. *A History of Greece*, 12 vols, London, 1846–56.
AMMOND, N. G. L. *A History of Greece to 332 BC*, Oxford, 1959.
ERODOTUS *The Histories*, trs. A. de Sélincourt, Harmondsworth, 1954.
OOD, S. *The Home of the Heroes: The Aegean Before the Greeks*, London, 1967.
UTARCH *Lives* in *The Rise and Fall of Athens. Nine Greek Lives*, trs. I. Scott-Kilvert, Harmondsworth, 1960.
ARN, W. *Hellenistic Civilization*, rev. ed. by Tarn and G. T. Griffith, London, 1952.
HUCYDIDES *The History of the Peloponnesian War*, trs. R. Warner, Harmondsworth, 1954.
ENOPHON *The Persian Expedition*, trs. R. Warner, Harmondsworth, 1949.
— *History of My Time*, trs. R. Warner, Harmondsworth, 1966.
MMERN, A. *The Greek Commonwealth*, Oxford, 1911.

List of Illustrations

The author and publishers are grateful to the many official bodies, institutions an individuals mentioned below for their assistance in supplying illustration material Illustrations without acknowledgement are from originals in the archives of Thame and Hudson. Thanks are particularly expressed to the Trustees of the British Museun for their courtesy in allowing the reproduction of illustrations 2, 5, 7, 8, 9, 14, 40, 42 44, 45, 47, 49, 51, 52, 57, 65, 70, 96, 100, 101 and 104.

5 Syracuse, dekadrachm, *c.* 480–479 BC. British Museum. Photo Brompton Studio

6 'Leonidas' statue. Sparta Museum

7 Bronze soldier. Courtesy of the Wadsworth Atheneum, Hartford, Conn.

8 Gorge of the Asopos. Photo Mary Burn

9 Arrowheads from Thermopylae

o Themistoclean stele from Troizen. Photo Alison Frantz

1 Athens, dekadrachm, *c.* 478 BC. British Museum. Photo Brompton Studio

2 Greek attacking Persian. Red-figure amphora from Rhodes. Metropolitan Museum of Art, Rogers Fund 1906

3 Serpent Column from Delphi at Constantinople. Photo German Archaeological Institute, Istanbul

4 Relief with practising gymnasts. National Museum, Athens

5 'Mourning Athena'. Acropolis Museum, Athens. Photo Max Hirmer

5 Bust of Pericles from Tivoli. British Museum

7 East front of the Parthenon. Photo Peter Clayton

8 Tree of Hippocrates, Cos. Photo Peter Clayton

9 Marble *kore* from the Acropolis. Acropolis Museum, Athens. Photo Max Hirmer

o Strangford Shield, detail. British Museum

101 Rider and soldier relief from the Parthenon. British Museum

102 Graffito on base of Athenian black glazed cup from Olympia. Olympia Museum. Photo German Archaeological Institute, Athens

103 Marble herm of Euripides. Mantua Museum

104 Marble statue of Socrates. British Museum

105 Nike statue by Paeonius of Mende. Olympia Museum. Photo German Archaeological Institute, Athens

106, 107 Spartan shield and its inscription from the Agora. Photo American School of Classical Studies, Athens

108 Farewell scene, red-figure crater. Ashmolean Museum, Oxford. Photo courtesy of the Director

109 Syracuse, dekadrachm signed by Euainetos, *c.* 395–380 BC. British Museum. Photo Brompton Studio

110 Chalcidian League, tetradrachm, *c.* 412–410 BC. British Museum. Photo Brompton Studio

111 Ceramicus, Athens. Photo Peter Clayton

112 Walls of Eleuthérai. Photo Mary Burn

113 Philip II, 359–336 BC, tetradrachm reverse. British Museum. Photo Brompton Studio

114 Demosthenes, Ashmolean Museum, Oxford. Photo courtesy of the Director

115 Alexander the Great. Detail of the 'Issus' mosaic. Naples Museum. Photo André Held

116 Darius III. Detail of the 'Issus' mosaic. Naples Museum. Photo André Held

117 Alexander the Great and Roxane. Onyx cameo. Kunsthistorisches Museum, Vienna. Photo Erwin Meyer

118 Lion of Chaeronea. Photo Max Hirmer

119 Macedonian and Persian. Detail 'Alexander sarcophagus'. Istanbul Museum. Photo Dieter Johannes

120 Map of Alexander's campaigns. Drawn by S. Schotten

121, 122 Alexander the Great, 336–323 BC, tetradrachm obverses. British Museum. Photos Brompton Studio

123 Alexander the Great, 336–323 BC, dekadrachm reverse. British Museum. Photo Brompton Studio

124 Seleucos I, 312–280 BC, tetradrachm obverse. British Museum. Photo Peter Clayton

125 Ptolemy I, 305–283 BC, tetradrachm obverse. British Museum. Photo Brompton Studio

126 Map of the 'Fetters of Greece'. Drawn by S. Schotten

127 Achaean League, tetradrachm, *c.* 370–360 BC. British Museum. Phot[o] Brompton Studio

128 Arcadian League, tetradrachm, *c*. 370–360 BC. British Museum. Phot[o] Brompton Studio

129 Seleucos I, 312–280 BC, tetradrachm reverse. British Museum. Phot[o] Brompton Studio

130 Antimachus, *c.* 180 BC, tetradrachm obverse. British Museum. Phot[o] Brompton Studio

131 Eucatrides, 170–165 BC, gold stater Bibliothèque Nationale, Paris

132 Menander of Bactria, tetradrachm obverse. British Museum. Phot[o] Brompton Studio

133 Demetrius of Bactria, 190–170 BC tetradrachm obverse. British Museum Photo Peter Clayton

134 T. Quinctius Flamininus, gold state[r] after 196 BC. Staatliche Museen z[u] Berlin

135 Pompey the Great, *c.* 50 BC. N[y] Carlsberg Glyptothek, Copenhagen

136 Cleopatra VII, 51–30 BC, coppe[r] British Museum. Photo Brompto[n] Studio

Index

Numbers in italics refer to illustrations